SECONDARY STARTERS AND PLENARIES
ENGLISH

Ready-to-use activities for teaching English

By Johnnie Young

BLOOMSBURY
LONDON • NEW DELHI • NEW YORK • SYDNEY

Published 2013 by Bloomsbury Education
Bloomsbury Publishing plc
50 Bedford Square, London, WC1B 3DP

www.bloomsbury.com

9781441199782

10 9 8 7 6 5 4 3 2 1

Typeset by Fakenham Prepress Solutions, Fakenham, Norfolk, NR21 8NN
Printed and bound by CPI Group (UK) Ltd, Croydon, CR0 4YY

This book is produced using paper that is made from wood grown in managed, sustainable
forests. It is natural, renewable and recyclable. The logging and manufacturing processes
conform to the environmental regulations of the country of origin.

Online resources accompany this book, available at:
www.bloomsbury.com/secondary-starters-and-plenaries-english-9781441199782

Please type the URL into your web browser and follow the instructions to access
the resources. If you experience any problems, please contact Bloomsbury at:
companionwebsites@bloomsbury.com

This book is dedicated to Duncan Burfoot, who I have been privileged to know for 54 years. Duncan has always been more than a friend to me; he is more like a brother.

Contents

Section 3: Reading fiction, poetry and drama

Section 4: Reading and writing: non-fiction

Section 5: Speaking and listening

Introduction

The importance of starters and plenaries

I have now been teaching for over 20 years and I have become more and more interested in the importance of engaging the students' attention effectively as soon as they enter the room and in ending the lesson in the best way possible.

In the thousands of lessons I have observed certain key problems are apparent. Firstly, in the understandable desire to engage the students quickly to ensure dynamic flow, the starters are often made easy to do. The problem here is that although this will engage the students it will not necessarily ensure good quality learning. This book includes carefully designed tasks, mostly available at three levels, supported by a whole range of materials developed to challenge and interest the students.

Plenaries are a special problem. All too often they are 'tagged on' at the end, made too easy and do not always consolidate the learning of the lesson in an interesting way. Why is this? There is an innate energy in a class as it approaches the end of the lesson. There is a powerful feel of inevitablitity as the group instinct comes into play and students prepare mentally to finish with the lesson. To try to interrupt that energy and get them to do a plenary is a surprisingly difficult thing to do. Many plenaries, in practice, are therefore a sort of hurried ritualistic routine which 'ticks a box' rather than being a meaningful activity. The students so often play the game and go through the motions in a flat uninspired way. The plenaries in this book directly address this problem. They work well because they are based on plenaries which have a track record of working well in practice and so help to redirect energy in inventive, creative and fun ways.

The benefits of these starters and plenaries

- They work well in practice: The teacher is helped every step of the way with detailed 'Teacher's tips' which explain clearly the best way to deliver based on the practice in the classroom.

- They link: The ideas are specially written so that the starter introduces the main part of the lesson and the plenary links everything together.

- They are interesting ideas: The ideas in this book have been selected because they have held the interest of students many times over. Many of the ideas involve unusual and innovative approaches.

- They engage students quickly but also challenge: The activities are designed to get the students working quickly and the range of support and prompt material is available to help ensure work flow.

- They help students reflect on their own learning: There are many opportunities in these activities for students to reflect on their own work and the work of their colleagues. They are designed to show that learning is a process rather than just an outcome. A lot of criteria for success checklists are provided to take the strain away from the teacher.

- They actively involve the students: Many of the activities require the students to get involved with reading, role play, presentations and reviewing each others' work.

- The are targeted: The topics selected are targeted to cover the key skills in English.

- Most of the activities are levelled: The activities are levelled as Easy, Medium and Challenging based around the core topic to allow the teacher to suitably and conveniently match the work to the appropriate ability. The level of the activity is signified using the following symbols:
  - **E** Easy
  - **M** Medium
  - **C** Challenging

The aim of this book

This book provides 25 starters and 25 plenaries, which link together and can be adapted to allow for the accommodation of a huge range of 'main courses' which can be included in the heart of the lesson.

The structure of the book and its levels

The book is divided into the five main areas of English:

Section 1: Writing

Key skills of developing vocabulary, writing to imagine, writing to advise and persuade and writing to describe are covered together with a focus on the use of diary writing skills and how that can help explore literature. Materials used include creative writing texts, role play scripts, letters and visualisation sessions. All of the activities in this section are offered at three levels except one of the fun plenaries for writing to persuade which involves the whole class in a dynamic and competitive way.

Section 2: Reading prose fiction

Here the focus includes understanding character, genre, narrator, setting mood and atmosphere, plot, story and theme. The section makes use of games, props, pictures and creative writing samples. Most of the activities are levelled except activities which lend themselves to a group dynamic.

Section 3: Reading fiction, poetry and drama

This section deals with rhyme, imagery, similies, metaphor dialogue and stagecraft. It makes use of a range of creative writing extracts and contains a strong comparative element as a key learning tool. Most of the activities are levelled except the few where the whole class involvement produces a better outcome.

Section 4: Reading and writing non-fiction

Here we have note taking skills, variety in non-fiction texts, features of non-fiction, and fact and opinion. Most of the activities here, because of the nature of the work, for example 'auction room,' are whole class activities rather than being levelled.

Section 5: Speaking and listening

This short but vital section includes whole class activities to ignite the skills of presentation, body language and debate.

How to use this book

Each starter comes with a linking plenary and is supported by materials for extra ideas, prompts and examples which are included in the book and as online printable worksheets and PowerPoints. There are also many useful criteria checklists so that the students can check their own work.

The teacher is carefully guided through how to deliver the work with detailed explanations and teacher's tips.

An important feature of the activities is encouraging students to feel comfortable to experiment with ideas and not to be afraid to try things out and fail. Failing is part of the process of learning and having the confidence to try again, the cornerstone of all learning, will be encouraged if you make everyone feel comfortable so that they can see and understand that what they are doing is part of a process rather than the end result.

There are lots of opportunities for students to present their findings to the class and this is seen as a very important part of the learning process. The way the teacher manages the feedback is also crucial for learning outcomes and plenty of advice is offered for that.

There is ample material and teachers may wish to adapt and cut down various parts for one starter and maybe come back to them on another day.

The timings are indicated in some important cases but generally are not specified as it depends on how the class deal with the individual activities as to whether the teacher cuts short or develops the work, in order to maintain interest and flow.

I would suggest that at the end of the lesson you ask your students what they thought of the starter and feedback activities and then adapt them for the next lesson accordingly. This process helps lead to better teaching and learning.

There are resources available online for you to use to prepare and run the starter or plenary, including PowerPoints and extra examples and resources. To access this material go to www.bloomsbury.com/secondary-starters-and-plenaries-english-9781441199782 and follow the instructions.

So here it is. 50 ideas distilled from 20 years of practice. I do hope they are useful to you and help you to continue to have great English lessons.

Acknowledgements

I would like to thank my publishers, Bloomsbury, and in particular Mel Wilson, Rosie Pattinson and Holly Gardner for their great advice and professionalism.

Johnnie Young

Section 1
Writing

Starter

A world of vocabulary

Useful for lessons when the objective is for students to extend their vocabulary with written exercises.

Explain to students that their vocabulary is all the different words which they know the meanings of and can use in their writing. The more they can increase that vocabulary, the more they can write in an engaging way and read with enhanced understanding, and therefore enjoy reading and writing more.

Give students a copy of 'A diary extract from *The Lost Island*' and read it to them.

A diary extract from *The Lost Island*

The island was thousands of miles from the nearest mainland. It was very **remote**. We had reached it the night before when our ship was wrecked on the rocks in the **tumultuous** storm. Now, at first light, after a bitterly cold night, our first thoughts were to find shelter and then work out a survival plan.

Tasks were **allocated** between the four of us: one was to collect wood for a signal fire; another was to find materials for shelter; a third was to **procure** something to eat and my **crucial** role was to find fresh water.

We set about our tasks with military **precision**. We all realised that our very survival depended on team work and **optimistic** thinking. There would be no room for negative thoughts at a time like this.

As we explored the island we discovered something very strange. In a deep valley we found seven enormous **sculptured** stone figures. They towered above us and were obviously **ancient**, judging by the **weathering** on the surface of the stone.

The really **intriguing** thing about them was what they were **depicted** as wearing. For the life of us they looked like space suits! How could that be if they were so old? My main desire now was to escape this island to safety so that we could return at some future time and study them in depth. How frightening and yet, at the same time, how incredibly exciting!

Activities

❺ Match up meanings

Prepare two sets of small cards for each pair of students. One set should have the key word and the other set should have the definitions. Jumble them up and then ask students, in pairs, to match up the words to their meanings.

Teacher's tips

If they find it difficult to match the cards, make it easier by indicating which paragraph the key word is in. Once they've matched them up successfully encourage students to work out ways to remember the meanings, perhaps by acting out a small scene for each word.

---

12 key words and definitions

1. **Remote**: situated far from a main area of population.

2. **Tumultuous**: making a loud and confused sound.

3. **Allocated**: distributed, or given out, in a certain way.

4. **Procure**: to obtain something by looking out carefully for it.

5. **Crucial**: something which is highly important to achieve success or failure.

6. **Precision**: with exactness and accuracy.

7. **Optimistic**: looking on the bright side about the outcome of something.

8. **Sculptured**: a three-dimensional model carved or made out of material like wood or stone.

9. **Ancient**: from the very distant past; very old.

10. **Weathering**: change the surface of something by long exposure to the weather.

11. **Intriguing**: arousing curiosity and fascination in something.

12. **Depicted**: represent something using a work of art.

Ⓜ Wanted: A word to fit this vacancy

Prepare two sets of cards for each pair of students. One set should have the key words and the other set should have a small piece of writing with a blank to fill with one of the key words. Jumble them up and ask the students to match them up. Sentence examples provided are below:

Wanted: A word to fit this vacancy

1. He sat wearing his summer shirt and bright blue shorts on his deckchair, sinking into the pure white sand and gazing into the _____ distance.

2. Eric ran as fast as he could. He hated being caught out in the middle of a field as dark storm clouds gathered. What was that? A blinding flash and then the most _____ crash as he dived for the ground with his hands on his head.

3. Great! Paintballing! What a wonderful birthday treat. The man in charge _____the rifles and a supply of paintballs to each of us.

4. I asked my mother why she had returned from the shops without the beef joint. She told me that the beef on offer in the supermarket was not up to her standards and she therefore planned to _____ a nice joint of beef tomorrow from her local butcher.

5. The pilot was having great difficulty seeing the runway in the mist as he brought the plane into land. He told the navigator that the readings from the altitude dials were _____ at this point.

6. After studying the uncut diamond for seven long hours the jeweller at last applied his hammer and chisel with great _____.

7. Our football team were four-nil down at half time but the captain was smiling. 'How can you smile at a time like this?' I asked.
'You must remain_____!' he replied. 'Otherwise we will certainly lose!'

8. Her face was so beautiful that it seemed to have been _____out of white marble by some great artist.

9. 'One of the mysteries of Stonehenge,' said the tour guide, 'is that nobody quite knows exactly how _____it really is.'

10. The woman ran her hand along the roof of the car, which was for sale, and frowned. She said: 'There does seem to have been quite a bit of _____ on this car. Has it been left outside a lot?'

11. Danny held his well wrapped birthday present with shaking hands. 'Look!' sighed Grandma. 'He finds the shape _____. I bet he can't wait to find out what it is!'

12. 'If you venture still further,' puffed the cave explorer, 'and look up at those strange lines you can just make out that the caveman _____ the shape of an ox.'

Teacher's answers

The sentence number	The matching word
1	remote
2	tumultuous
3	allocated
4	procure
5	crucial
6	precision
7	optimistic
8	sculptured
9	ancient
10	weathering
11	intriguing
12	depicted

❸ The 12 word challenge

Provide the students with a list of the 12 key words and a list of writing tasks (examples on the next page). Ask them to pick one task and write it out using as many of the 12 words as possible.

Choices of short writing tasks

1. *Gone shopping.* You have had a great day shopping with a friend and you write a letter to another friend explaining what a great day you had.

2. *Love poem.* You have met the love of your life. Write a poem about it.

3. *Visualise the future.* Imagine that you have achieved your ideal job or career some time in the future. Write a diary of 'one day in the life' describing what it is like.

4. *Speech.* You have won a competition to go on TV and deliver a short speech about something you feel passionate about. Write that short speech.

5. *Feeling down.* A person you know well has had a lot of bad luck lately and is feeling down. Write a letter of encouragement to try to cheer them up.

Teacher's tips

• Provided online is an example of openers for each writing task together with a full example of one of the tasks using all the 12 words. If the students find it difficult to start writing, show them a sample answer. Tell them that they don't have to use all the words, just as many as they can, and they can use them in any order they wish to. If they really struggle, tell them they can use the sample writing openers and continue them if they would prefer.

• Students can change the form of the words to fit the sense if they want to. So 'intriguing' can be changed to 'intriguingly'.

Plenary

Reflecting on the vocabulary they have learnt

Based on the new words the students have learnt today in their work, allocate the appropriate task from the list below.

Activities

ⓔ Ways to remember new words

Ask students to write out the new words they have learnt today together with their meanings. Ask them to discuss ways of remembering the words and their meanings.

ⓜ Wanted poster

Ask students to select a particular new word they have learnt today and to design a wanted poster for it (see 'Wanted poster template'). Encourage students to creatively play around with the idea to mimic the presentation of a wanted poster. There is an example of a completed wanted poster online.

Wanted poster template

WANTED

THE WORD

Could be found under the guise of: *(students to look up other forms of the word in a dictionary)*

Physical description: *(maybe give the consonant/vowel pattern of the word)*

Arch enemy: *(students to look up a word, if possible, which is opposite in meaning)*

Usually can be tracked down in conversations where someone is trying to: *(students to give an example of conversation where this word is likely to be used)*

This word's history can be traced back to: *(look up the history of the word)*

Large reward offered

---

❻ Selling the word

Ask students to select a particular new word they have learnt today and sketch out an advert designed to sell the word. An example is provided online.

Teacher's tip

The ideas for the poster and advert work well to anchor the new word in the memory. They are fun. Show the students the examples online to give them the general idea and then offer a few suggestions. You will find that they sometimes have trouble responding to unfamiliar words but encourage them to be adventurous and to experiment. Remind them that if they try to stretch themselves a little and be creative the information will stick firmly in their memory and help their understanding.

Starter

Writing to imagine

Ideal for lessons where the objective is to write imaginatively.

Show the students the text *Herbert's house* and read it with them.

Herbert's house

Herbert, a likeable man, but, it has to be said, a man of very strange ideas, had spent the last seven years working hard, building his own 'dream house' on a plot of land he had purchased smack bang in the centre of a busy town.

As the house had progressed Herbert had felt prouder and prouder but, because he was so busy, he hadn't noticed the comments that neighbours were making. Comments like 'What does he think he's playing at? That's the strangest house I've ever seen!' Or 'How on earth did he get planning permission for something as weird as that?' Someone even commented 'It's dangerous that is. When people drive by they get distracted. No one can believe it's true!'

At last it was finished and Herbert excitedly spent his first night in his new house. He had not used builders at all but had done everything himself. That's one of the reasons it took so long to build. Another thing was that it had now taken every single penny of his considerable savings.

The next day Herbert was surprised to be woken abruptly by a sharp rat-a-tat-tat on his door. You see, what Herbert hadn't realised was that although he had worked 16 hour days for seven years, and although, in his mind, the design was 'amazing', he hadn't in fact got planning permission and therefore he found himself, in his pyjamas face to face with a burly senior official from the local council who held out an official looking letter. Herbert read the letter. To his utter dismay and surprise it stated that because there was no planning permission, and because it was so strange and unusual, the house was to be demolished within 28 days!

Activities

➊ Answering questions imaginatively

Ask students to answer the questions, in sentences or notes, to build up an imaginative idea of what the house may have looked like.

Questions about Herbert's house

1. What colour was the roof?

2. What material were the walls made of?

3. What was strange about the chimney?

4. Why were the windows so unusual?

5. What was it about the front door that caused so much attention?

6. What did it have in the garden that surprised people so much?

7. How was the fence odd?

8. What didn't you expect to see instead of a shed?

9. What surprised you that Herbert had installed instead of drain pipes?

10. Why did people gasp when they went round to the back of the house?

Teacher's tip

A great feedback exercise for this activity is to form a circle of ten students, with you standing in the centre. You should call out the questions quickly and point to different students for answers.

➍ Complete the sentence

Display the 'Complete the sentence' worksheet. Ask them to copy and complete the sentences about the house.

Complete the sentence

1. One neighbour was so angry with the house that she …

2. It was the statue in the front garden which caused most comments because it was …

3. On the roof was a bizarre attempt at energy saving. Herbert had fitted a …

4. I don't know how the postman was supposed to deliver any letters because …

5. Apparently Herbert had wanted to have ivy on the walls. Because that took so long to grow, instead of ivy he used …

6. It appeared that Herbert wanted his own gym attached to the house. Unfortunately, instead of a gym he had …

7. Looking at the house it was quite clear that Herbert liked sailing because …

8. He may have been an animal lover but the cat flap was ridiculous. Let me describe it. It was …

9. Herbert had thought of a very original way of putting his rubbish out. What he did was to …

10 I've heard of alternative types of kitchen but Herbert's kitchen was perhaps one step too far. Let me try to describe it to you. It had …

❸ Write a description

Ask students to write an imaginative description of Herbert's house making it as unusual and interesting as possible.

Teacher's tip

If students struggle to get started, provide them with the following opener and tell them to continue the description:

As I got closer to the house I could not believe what I was seeing. First of all, it seemed to be leaning over, at an angle, and I was quite surprised that it hadn't actually fallen over! The next thing that struck me as odd was …

Plenary

Reflecting on writing to imagine

Materials required: highlighter pens.

Activities

🄴 Highlighter pens

Ask students to work in pairs and look at each others' work. Invite them to highlight parts of their partner's work in the following way:

1. Blue: parts which are good.

2. Green: parts which could possibly be taken out.

3. Pink: parts which could be improved on.

🄼 Suggestions for improvements

Ask students to review each others' work and find one part which could be improved. They can then write out ideas explaining how the work might be improved.

🄲 Re-writing to improve

Ask students to review each others' work and find one part which could be improved. The student then rewrites that part to enhance its effectiveness.

Teacher's tip

Give all of the students the 'Criteria for improving creative and imaginative writing' on the next page and encourage them to use it to help them suggest specific ideas and improvements.

Criteria for improving creative and imaginative writing

1. Are the sentences nice and clear?

2. Has a good choice of interesting vocabulary been used?

3. Are specific details described?

4. Are there some good strong visual images?

5. Is there a story line which keeps the writing moving forward?

Starter

Writing to argue and persuade

Just right to start off a lesson where the focus is writing to argue or persuade, or reading texts which argue and persuade.

Ask the class to imagine that one of the students was attacked on the way home one night and a meeting is called the next day. The result of the meeting will be to write a letter to persuade the headteacher to adopt an idea the students have come up with.

Arrange for students to read the 'What happened last night' mini play in groups of five: A: Student 1 (the victim); B: Student 2 (a friend); C: Teacher; D: Mother of student 1; E: Police officer.

What happened last night

A meeting has been arranged at the school.

C: Thank you all for coming to discuss this unfortunate event. Perhaps we could start. If you could run through again exactly what happened and what your thoughts and feelings are?

A: (*still slightly upset and shaken.*) Well, as I've told the police already, I was walking home last night, on my own and I cut through Turpin's Alley, to take a short ...

D: How many times have I told you not to go down that dangerous alley on your own?

A: Yes mum, I know, I know... (*tuts and pulls a face*) when a guy jumped out and tried to take my mobile out of my hand. I struggled with him and he knocked me to the ground and then prised the phone out of my hand. Then he went to punch me but I managed to dodge his fist and he ran off. It was horrible! (*Puts her head in her hands and gets upset.*)

D: You were very, shaken my poor dear, weren't you? Look, don't get upset, we're going to sort this out.

A: Yes. It was just a horrible experience.
(*Short pause during which everyone looks at each other awkwardly*)

E: Don't you worry miss. We've taken a good description from you and my people are searching for the culprit right now. We'll catch him, don't you worry!

B: Thank you officer, but my friend and I think that something more should be done. We think that it is time for self-defence lessons to be held at school as part of the curriculum. This is not the first attack. There have been many recently. We've got to do something about it.

C: What is the law at the moment regarding self-defence, officer?

E: Basically, the law states that an individual has the right to use reasonable force to defend him or herself or others, if faced with a physical attack.

C: You don't think it would make some of the students a bit aggressive, do you?

E: No, I don't think so. A good instructor should teach that self-defence is a last resort and generally encourages people to live peaceful lives.

C: I'll have a word with the headteacher about it.

D: I suppose he will be concerned about the cost of it?

C: Yes, I think that will probably be one of the considerations.

A: I feel so strongly about this that I am going to write to the headteacher myself and put with it a petition with as many signatures as I can get.

C: What a good idea. I hope you're successful in persuading him.

Activities

❺ Write a list

Ask students to write a list of reasons for having self-defence classes at the school and then a list of possible objections which may be raised.

Teacher's tip

If students have problems coming up with original ideas then show them the 'For and against list' on the next page and ask them to rank the items in order of importance.

For and against list

For:

1. Students will feel safer.

2. Students will have more confidence and self esteem (a confident walk discourages an attack).

3. Students will think more strategically to avoid high risk situations.

4. There will be the satisfaction of knowing that something positive is being done to try to improve the situation.

Against:

1. It could be argued that teaching students self-defence techniques might make the playground scuffles more dangerous and encourage students to be violent.

2. Parents may not go along with it.

3. It might give students an exaggerated idea of their safety.

4. The costs would be high.

ⓜ Come up with some sentences

Ask students to work in pairs and come up with some sentences which could go into the letter to persuade the headteacher to agree with the students' way of thinking.

Teacher's tip

Show students 'Techniques for writing persuasively' to give them ideas about what might go into the letter. Tell them not to worry at this stage about the structure of the letter but to just write sentences which are persuasive and could be used in the letter.

Techniques for writing persuasively

1. A first-hand account of something that happened. In this case the student being attacked.

2. Find an area that the persuader and the person being persuaded both agree on. In this case both the headteacher and the students want the students to be safe.

3. Use reasonable argument. Show the logic of the argument.

4. Remember that people have a sense of right and wrong and you must show that your idea is right and fair. It can be shown in this case how unfair it is for someone to hurt someone and get away with it.

5. With care, add feelings and passion. In this case the student was hurt and this of course causes powerful feelings which can be used to help persuade.

❸ The structure of the letter

Ask students to work in groups and write out a structure for the proposed letter with notes for the paragraph plan. Tell them they won't have time to write the letter itself, just to note the order in which the points will be made.

Teacher's tips

If the students have trouble starting, give them the 'Jumbled paragraph plan' and ask them to put it in order. Once they have the right order, it works well for the students to line up at the front of the class, in that order, with each one representing a particular paragraph. They then tell the class, in sequence, what their particular paragraph will say. There is an example of a finished letter online.

Jumbled paragraph plan

- a passionate rousing call to action

- the proposed solution and its benefits

- states when change should happen – reinforcement, persuasive tool – petition

- the problem stated by way of an anecdote

- use of compelling statistics and an appeal for common ground

- anticipates obstacles and tackles them

Plenary

Reflecting on writing to argue and persuade

Activity

Divide the class into four groups and ask each group to stand in a line against the four walls of the room. Allocate them a group letter: A, B, C and D. Have a chart on the board clearly labelled A, B, C and D ready for the scores. Explain that they are going to have a quick fire competition to see which group can get the most points for effective use of persuasive language.

Display the five core persuasive techniques for all the students to see.

The five core persuasive techniques

1. A first-hand account of something that happened.

2. An area that the persuader and the person being persuaded both agree on.

3. Reasonable, logical argument.

4. Show that your idea is right and fair.

5. Feelings and passion.

Use the PowerPoint provided online which contains ten statements. Show the students the first statement. One person from each group has to give a persuasive reason to support, or disagree with the statement. You can use the PowerPoint for several rounds of the game. Students may use a technique from the list of five core techniques, or they may well think up a technique themselves. The teacher awards points in accordance with how persuasive the language used is. All the answers will be spoken, rather than written, for the purposes of the competition, and to keep the pace brisk.

Teacher's tips

- This plenary works well because, although all the class are involved, by standing in groups, only those feeling confident and comfortable will actively participate on behalf of their groups.

- A worked example of the sort of things which might be said is shown online. This can be shared with the students to give them an idea of the way the competition works as it includes the teacher's responses.

Starter

Writing to advise

A great way to start the lesson when the objective is to practice writing to advise.

Split the students into groups of three and read them the 'Letter seeking advice', explaining to them it is a letter written by a teenager addressed to a magazine, seeking advice.

Letter seeking advice

Dear Sir/Madam,

I badly needed some money to go on a school trip because my parents could not afford it. I have a very trusting neighbour and I go in to see her now and again. She is an elderly lady. Yesterday, as I was making her tea in the kitchen, and she was in the lounge, I noticed her open handbag and a large amount of cash. I'm afraid that temptation got the better of me and I stole £100. The problem is I've been up all night worrying about it. If my parents find out they'll go mad. I feel terrible that I've betrayed such a trusting and kind neighbour. But, I also have a burning desire to go on the school trip (three days in France) because my boyfriend is going and I'm worried that he might go off with someone else if I'm not there. I write to you as a desperate act of last resort. What should I do?

Please help.

Activities

❸ List advice

Ask students to make a list of any advice that they can think of which would be suitable to include in a letter of reply.

Teacher's tips

If students find it hard to think of ideas show them the 'Possible issues involved' list to encourage ideas.

Possible issues involved:

1. Could she put the money back into the neighbour's handbag next time she visits?

2. Could she tell her parents the whole thing?

3. Could she tell her boyfriend the whole thing?

4. Is there some other honest way of getting the money for the trip?

5. Could she return the money and then ask the neighbour for a loan and do jobs around the house to pay it back over time?

6. Could she put the money back and would it be so bad if she didn't go on the trip? Is she worrying too much about her boyfriend?

Ⓜ Compare to checklist

Ask students to write down as many bits of advice that they can think of in the time allowed and then compare their advice to the checklist of 'Features of writing to advise'. Tell them they should use the list to see if they can make any changes and improvements to their own ideas in preparation for writing a letter of reply.

Features of writing to advise

1. Does the advice consider who the audience is?

2. Does the advice offer a range of sensible and reasonable ideas?

3. Is the delivery of the advice friendly?

4. Does the advice sound as if it has come from someone who has experience?

5. Does the advice, if taken, solve the problem?

6. Is the advice clear and easy to follow?

7. Does the person giving the advice indicate that they empathise (understand) with the problem?

8. Does the advice show that a lot of thinking and care has gone into it?

9. If sentences of advice have been written are they in an appropriate style (ideally formal with some informal expressions used?)

❸ Form some sentences

Ask the students to write a list of all the advice they can think of, then to develop the list into sentences which could be included in a letter of reply. They are then to compare their sentences with the checklist 'Features of writing to advise' to see if they can make any improvements.

Plenary

Reflecting on writing to advise

Use this plenary after students have written a letter or piece of writing offering advice. In pairs get them to swap their letters and to review each other's work.

Activities

Ⓔ Highlight features

Ask students to highlight parts of the letter that appear on the 'Features of writing to advise' checklist (see page 22).

ⓜ Identify and comment on areas to improve

Ask students to highlight parts of the letter that they think could be improved. Then, referring to the 'Features of writing to advise' checklist, ask them to make brief comments on what improvements could be made.

Ⓖ Identify and improve

Ask students to highlight parts of the letter that they think could be improved. Then, referring to the 'Features of writing to advise' checklist, they are to experiment re-writing small extracts to show how improvements could be made.

Teacher's tip

It is a good idea to tie things up with a quick bit of feedback using examples from students' work. Your main aim should be to create an atmosphere of discovery where the process of helping each other and constantly improving is prominent, rather than the focus being on correct end results.

Starter

Writing to describe

Perfect to engage and prepare the students with a small descriptive writing exercise when the main body of the lesson is to write an extended piece of descriptive writing.

The aim of this activity is for students to imagine something in the future and then describe it as clearly as they can. Play some soft relaxing music (I recommend Mahler Symphony no. 5 – the slow movement). As they relax, read them 'Your future garden'.

Your future garden

'I want you to try something now. Just relax and calm your breathing and listen to the music. I want you to imagine something and to do that you have to clear your mind. Are you ready? Now, in many years from now, shall we say 12, you may well have a job, a family and your own home together with pets and maybe an assortment of possessions.

Now I want you to imagine that you had always wanted a garden designed to your own idea of perfection. Imagine that you are standing at the front of your home. It is a hot, sunny day and you are feeling at peace with the world and at peace with your life so far. Everything is going fine. Now walk slowly up to the house and open the front door. Go in. What colours have you used to decorate it with? Move from room to room. Look at the furniture. Look at your possessions.

Outside you are so pleased with the large secluded garden that has taken you years to get exactly as you want it. Now, imagine you are sitting on one of those soft sun loungers that you just sink back into and someone brings you your favourite drink. Sit and relax and look at your wonderful garden and as you describe it get up and slowly walk around it, and because you are in such a peaceful mood you notice the details of things as if for the first time …'

Teacher's tip

The choice of music for this activity is important. It is difficult to get everybody to like the same music so I usually just put the music on and let it play and when you get comments like 'Can't we have something more modern?' or 'This is funeral music', just gently deflect the comment with 'Maybe next time we'll play something different. But for now I'd like to just try this one please. Just let it flow for a little while …' The students then soon settle and listen.

Activities

ⓔ The range of things you would find

Ask students to write down as many things as they can think of that they might find in the garden. When they have done that, get them to go back over the list and jot down small descriptions of the things.

> ### Teacher's tip
>
> If students have trouble getting started, show them the 'Description examples' list below which includes examples of small descriptions to prompt their ideas and make their descriptions interesting.

Description examples

Things usually found in a garden	Small descriptions
A bridge over a pond	Made of wood and reflecting like a ghost in the water
Flowers	Soft yellow with a small insect clambering on it
Mossy undergrowth	Like a miniature forest beneath your feet (simile)
Dew	Globules of silver
Mist	Like the veil of a ghostly bride
A fork leaning against the shed	Reminding me of my granddad who was often working in his garden
A statue	Weathered with a small robin sitting on it

ⓜ Complete the description

Ask students to complete the sentences in 'My garden in the early morning' to build up a description of their dream garden.

My garden in the early morning

I stand here in the ....

The dew is still heavy on the grass and as I crouch down and look ...

I love this garden of mine. All these years to get it designed and laid out just right. The small lake has a bridge which is...

Curling over the edge of the water are ...

I wander over, with bare feet, on the spongy grass and gently smell ...

Listen. I can hear the small sounds of birds and tiny rustlings in the undergrowth. Looking over to the far edge of borders are a ...

I follow the edge of the water and come to the small waterfall where ...

Teacher's tip

Encourage students to be imaginative and not to restrict themselves to the sentences provided but to come up with some of their own too. It is a good idea when they have completed their writing to compare what they have done to the example of a finished piece. There is one provided online.

ⓒ Writing a full description

Ask students to use the 'Idea prompts' checklist to help them write an interesting description of their own.

Idea prompts

1. Put yourself in the picture and move around to get different views on things.

2. What time of day is it?

3. What is the temperature like?

4. Put touch into your description – not just your hands but maybe your bare feet.

5. Add smells and scents.

6. Include sounds both far away and close up.

7. Describe close up things but also far away things as impressions.

8. At times in your description look closely at something and describe the details.

9. Include similes to bring the language alive – but not too many.

10. Use carefully thought out adjectives but again, not too many.

11. Introduce interesting words into your description.

12. Are there reflections?

13. Make interesting use of colours by combining them.

14. What do certain things remind you of?

15. Include actions where you can as things change in your description.

Teacher's tip

Very often with this exercise the students follow the checklist so closely that their written work reads like a list of sentences. Online there is a finished example of a description based on the checklist. Show this to students so they can see how the ideas are connected together. It is a good idea to let them have a go with their own writing first and then compare it to the example. If they get time they could then edit and improve the connecting phrases.

Plenary

Reflecting on writing to describe

These tasks are designed to be applied to the piece of written work completed in the main part of the lesson.

Activities

ⓔ Review to improve

In pairs, ask students to swap their piece of descriptive writing and compare it to the 'Ideas prompts' checklist (on page 28) to see if there are things which could have been added. Then ask students to write out examples of what could have been added to enhance the writing.

Ⓜ Review to give an opinion

Ask students to review their partner's descriptive work and then highlight three areas: two which they like and one which they feel could be improved. Then ask them to describe the reasons why they have made these decisions.

Teacher's tip

It is particularly difficult for some students to write substantial comments about why they actually like something. The key is to find specific things they can say and then match to the work they are reviewing. The 'Idea prompts' checklist (on page 28) will help them focus in with this work.

ⓖ Write extracts to improve

Ask students to review each others' work and then select three examples which could be extended or improved. Ask students to re-write small examples to show exactly how they could be improved and then discuss this with their partners.

Starter

Writing diaries to explore characters in literature

Ideal when you want students to explore characters in literature by putting themselves into the story and a specific character's shoes, using the diary form.

Explain to students that diaries are personal intimate pieces of writing which reveal private thoughts and feelings – reading them helps us to gain a greater understanding of a character.

Provide students with the following list of a diary entries.

Diary entries

1. **The catwalk fashion parade in Rome**
   How about that! Today was such a great day for me. Who would have thought that I would win such a great prize? I've been taken to lunch at a top restaurant with a top fashion designer and then given a prime seat to watch the world class fashion show. Then the highlight! My chance to actually go on the catwalk myself wearing a specially designed dress…

2. **My first weekend job – working in a busy café**
   Well – what a day! I'm going to record it all in my diary while it is still fresh in my mind. My first day of work – a weekend job in a busy café. The boss was nice and understanding and the customers seemed to know I was new and were patient. I suppose the highlights of the day (both good and bad) were…

3. **My first date**
   We decided to go and see a movie and although it's now late and I'm tired I've decided to write it all down in my diary while it's still fresh in my mind. I don't want to lose any of it because it turned out to be, unexpectedly, the funniest time of my life. The first thing that happened was…

4. **The inheritance**
   The letter arrived yesterday and from this day on I intend to write in my diary every single day to record how my life will go from now on. Dear old Great Uncle Bernard. I had no idea he was so rich. And to leave most of it to me! It's more than a lottery jackpot. Already great changes are happening in my life. For example…

5. **Lost**

Now that I'm back, safe and sound (almost) and recovering nicely in hospital (and because I'm so bored) I thought I would put pen to paper and record the events of the last few days. It still seems quite hard to believe that all those strange things could have happened to me and maybe if I write it all down it will somehow make more sense. We were on holiday in Dartmoor when I decided it would be a good idea to explore around a bit on my own. I think I would have been alright if that thick fog hadn't descended on me like that. I ended up getting totally lost. I first saw the old house as a blurred dark shape emerging out of the fog but as I got closer...

Activities

ⓔ What might happen next?

Ask students to pick one of the diary entries and to jot down notes about the sorts of things that might be included in the next part of the entry.

ⓜ Continue the diary entry

Ask students to pick an entry and to continue it in the style that it is written.

ⓖ Write your own diary entry

Ask students to choose a scenario from the list below and then write their own diary entry expressing the thoughts and feelings they might have if they were the character in the scenario.

Choose a scenario

1. You were invited to a friend's for tea but had a spectacular accident. Although you didn't get hurt yourself, you did cause a great deal of damage to your friend's place.

2. You were in the library with a friend and because you got bored you played a small prank which unfortunately went horribly wrong.

3. Your hero big brother has just arrived home after travelling round the world in the Royal Navy. You have been looking forward to this moment for a long time.

4. You can't stop thinking about the person you met in the summer who has now gone back to his/her home in Australia.

5. Most of your life you had trouble making friends but two weeks ago you confided in your grandad. He gave you some great advice and since then you've been using it and to your amazement and joy you are now starting to make some really great friends.

6. You wanted to be a hair stylist but after your eventful work experience you have completely changed your mind.

7. You had lately felt a little hard done by and thought that you were an unlucky sort of person and generally not pleased with the hand that life had dealt you. That was until you made that visit and now you feel not just lucky but ashamed of yourself for thinking that you weren't a lucky person.

Teacher's tip

It helps to get the students started by discussing their choice with them and then getting them to imagine the different possibilities of the scenario. Next, get them to think about what their own reactions to the scenario would be and encourage them to discuss how they feel, with their partner writing down the thoughts as they speak them.

Plenary

Applying writing diaries to explore specific literature

Ask students to choose a character in the text they have been studying in today's lesson and a particular point in the story. Ask students to imagine that they are that character.

Activities

E Guided character's diary

Ask students to complete the gaps.

Complete the gaps

'When I look around this place the main things I notice are_____. Thinking over the events of today the ones that stand out for me are_____ and this is because_____. The person who I think I like the most is _____ and this is probably because_____. The person I really don't like is _____and the reason is because_____ . The food and drink I had today included_____. As I write this diary note I caught a glimpse of myself in the mirror and because I think it will be interesting for me to read in years to come, I shall describe my appearance:_____.

Teacher's tip

Remind the students that the short gaps do not mean one word fillers. Encourage them to write as much as they want. Remind them that material for their diary might not be obvious in the text they have studied but they must imagine things themselves from clues in the text.

M 'What if?' scenarios

Ask students to choose one of the 'What if?' scenarios and then consider how the character they have chosen would react, then to continue the diary note.

What if?

1. I was unexpectedly given a large sum of money today. Now I shall be able to…

2. So I have been granted the magic wish have I? I can now make one of the characters disappear forever! The one I shall choose is…

Teacher's tip

With this activity there is a danger of the student writing a very short response, so actively encourage them to discuss the work and what they have been reading with their partner before they write. Ask them to develop and expand their thoughts in writing as much as they can.

⑥ Right in the middle of the action

Ask students to pick a point in time right in the middle of the action of the story that they have been reading today. They are then to imagine that the action is frozen in time and that they are a secret observer and must write a private diary entry recording all they see and their reaction to it.

If the students have trouble starting, show them this example based on a well known story to give them an idea of how it might be done.

A Christmas Carol

A Christmas Carol: frozen at the point where The Ghost of Christmas Yet to Come points a bony finger.

The characters around me seem frozen in time. There is a huge dark form standing like a giant monk in black robes pointing a sinister white bony finger into the distance. I'm actually feeling quite scared to stand so close to him. We seem to be in a graveyard. The light is dim and gloomy. A few metres away is the frozen form of a thin haunted looking man with night clothes on. His face is bony and wrinkled. The thing that strikes me most is the stare in his eyes. I follow that stare and walk a few paces towards a gravestone. On it are the words: 'Ebenezer Scrooge'.

Section 2
Reading prose fiction

Starter

Understanding character

Perfect for lessons on exploring characters in plays and prose.

Explain to the students that when a writer of fiction creates a character, they are trying to make the person both interesting and believable. To understand characters in fiction we can consider many factors including those listed on the 'Understanding character' checklist.

Understanding character

1. Their possessions and the things you might find in their pockets.

2. The way they are physically described.

3. The thoughts they have.

4. The actions they take.

5. The things which motivate them.

6. The way they speak and the things they say.

7. The way they are treated by others and the way they behave towards other people.

Activities

⑤ Write a list

Tell students that it is useful to consider what sorts of things various characters might carry in their pockets as these items could provide intriguing clues when we are trying to understand them. Ask students to name three items which might be found in each of the following character's pockets:

1. a middle-aged newspaper reporter who travels abroad a lot

2. an artist

3. an actor

4. a racing driver

5. a hairdresser

6. a taxi driver

Ask students to think of both obvious and not so obvious items and say they must be prepared to explain their ideas. Tell them it may be useful to think about what things the characters need with them for their jobs but also things that tell us about their private lives.

Teacher's tip

With less able students it helps to suggest a couple of items to get them engaged. For example, 'The reporter would probably have a map and a passport. What else?'

Ⓜ Next steps

Ask students to read the following extract and explain, in writing, what they think the character will do next:

Next steps

'She was not enjoying her school trip to such an icy cold country. Back at home she could cause trouble and continue with her furtive and troublemaking actions. Here she was being watched. So what was so special, she thought, about this ice sculpture anyway? So what, if it had taken the artist ten days of careful work! There were lots of delicately carved bits. She looked around. Nobody was watching her at this particular moment...'

Teacher's tip

To generate interesting ideas, get students to work in pairs and jot down key note 'what ifs?' If they need a prompt for this suggest the following 'What ifs' and ask them to continue that idea.

What if?

a) She does not get noticed as she breaks up the ice sculpture but this leads to her doing more and more serious vandalism until it gets totally out of control? What could her escalating vandalism be?

b) She does get caught? What would be her punishment and how would she react to it?

c) She vandalises it in such a way that she unexpectedly gets hurt? In detail, what happens and what new information does that reveal about her character in the way she reacts?

Ⓒ Motivations

Tell students that if a character came from a very poor background, it might be the case that he strives to acquire as much money as he can in order to protect himself from returning to the horrors of poverty. Ask students to list other types of situations which might motivate a character and become the 'driving force' of their life.

Teacher's tip

If the students cannot think of their own idea for a driving force suggest the following which they can then develop in more detail:

a) A character feels inferior to his big brother and starts doing things to try change and change this dynamic and start to feel superior. What could those things be?

b) A character was badly bullied as a child. He sets out on a plan of action which will prevent him ever being bullied again. What might that be?

c) A character, as a child, was ignored by everyone. What might she do that, from now on, would place her at the centre of everyone's attention?

Plenary

Applying the understanding of character

Ask the students to think about the characters they have studied in the main part of the lesson.

Activities

❺ What is in his pocket?

Think about a character in the book you are studying. List three things that are likely to be in his pocket. Explain how those items might link to what we know about that character and could help us to understand the character more.

> **Teacher's tip**
>
> A good way to get students working on this is to think of a moment in the a plot when their chosen character did something. Encourage them to focus in on the detail of an object they would have needed and describe it in detail, even for such a casual thing as, for example, looking at their watch. What type of watch would it be to match the character? A strong powerful man, for example, may well have a strong sturdy watch.

ⓜ The character's description

Pick one character in the book you have been studying and read the description given by the author. What is the most important part of the description and why? Try to add some details of your own to the description.

> **Teacher's tip**
>
> Remind students to make use of the 'Understanding character' checklist (on page 37) to imaginatively fill in the gaps not given by the author. Encourage the students to get into the habit of asking questions like 'What might they have been wearing' and so on.

⊙ Character's thoughts

Ask students to select a particular moment in the story they are reading and write out the thoughts that the character could be having at that time, in addition to what it actually says in the text. How does this help us understand the character?

A good way to encourage students to tackle this is to select a small dramatic moment from the work and then to get them to focus on what is actually being said. Get them to read it through a couple of times and then apply a set of questions:

1. What mood would she be in at this point and why?

2. Is her appearance at this point fresh or tired?

3. What is she holding in her hand as she says these words?

4. What would be the tension in her body – relaxed or up tight?

5. Where would she be looking?

6. What sounds would she be focussing on?

Then, equipped with this information the student can write out an 'internal monologue' of the character's private thoughts in the format below.

Internal monologue

This example is set in Shakespeare's *Romeo and Juliet*, at the moment when Juliet first sets eyes on Romeo.

'He looks so calm and lovely. My heart is strangely beating fast and the loud music seems to have quietened, in my mind. The dancing people are fading all around into a grey blur. The small purse in my hand is being clutched with increasing tension. Why are my hands damp? Is it sweat? I know my face in reddening and I just caught a glimpse of my eyes in a mirror. They are alive with sparkle. What is happening to me?'

Starter

Looking at types of genres

Just right for lessons which focus on the different types of genre in prose fiction.

Explain to students that you are going to start the lesson with a genre game. Divide the class in half. The first half should stand at the front and call out from their 'Genre clues information sheet' (on the next page). The second half of the class remain seated and enter numbers on their 'Genre score sheets' in the appropriate boxes. At the end the points can be added up.

Genre score sheet

Genre	Typical objects which usually appear in these types of story	Typical characters who usually appear in these types of story	Typical events which usually appear in these types of story
Western			
Ghost			
Horror			
Comedy			
Murder Mystery and Detective			
Romance			
Sci fi			
Thriller			
Travel			
War			

Teacher's tip

This works very well if you oversee and direct proceedings by getting the students at the front to call out the clues in number sequence. The 'Genre clues information sheet' contains 30 clues which can be divided up among the students. Make sure they emphasise the number of the clue and don't read out the clues too quickly. If students writing down the numbers have trouble categorising a particular clue, slow things down and give them some tips to help them out, although don't linger on one clue for too long because you should keep the pace brisk.

Genre clues information sheet

TO = *Typical objects which usually appear in these types of story*

TC = *Typical characters who usually appear in these types of story*

TE = *Typical events which usually appear in these types of story*

1. (TO) The full moon.

2. (TO) A custard pie (to go in someone's face).

3. (TO) A magnifying glass.

4. (TO) A map.

5. (TO) Spurs on the boots.

6. (TO) A coffin.

7. (TO) A box of chocolates.

8. (TO) A flying saucer.

9. (TO) A coded message.

10. (TO) A machine gun.

11. (TC) Strange creatures with blue skin and bulging eyes and thin necks.

12. (TC) The sheriff.

13. (TC) Someone wrongly accused and on the run.

14. (TC) A shadowy vision.

15. (TC) A mad scientist intent on evil experiments.

16. (TC) A brave soldier.

17. (TC) A person who seems to get involved in a lot of minor accidents.

18. (TC) Someone who loves visiting new places all the time.

19. (TC) A clever police officer.

20. (TC) A beautiful young woman.

21. (TE) A body is found dead in the library.

22. (TE) The town's bank is raided and a posse is called together to look for the bandits.

23. (TE) A visitor knocks on the door of an old deserted house.

24. (TE) Someone looks around the room at a party and looks lovingly into another person's eyes.

25. (TE) A train breaks down on a long trek through a desert region.

26. (TE) The terrified victim sees, cast onto the wall, the shadowy outline of an axe being raised in the air.

27. (TE) Someone runs round a corner and collides with someone who is carrying lots of things which spill out all over the place.

28. (TE) A bright light appears in the sky and electricity is drained from peoples' cars.

29. (TE) Someone dodges into a doorway and peeps behind to see that he is being followed.

30. (TE) Despite heavy cross fire a soldier runs across the field to rescue his injured friend.

Teacher's answers

Genre	Typical objects which usually appear in these types of story	Typical characters who usually appear in these types of story	Typical events which usually appear in these types of story
Western	5	12	22
Ghost	1	14	23
Horror	6	15	26
Comedy	2	17	27
Murder Mystery and Detective	3	19	21
Romance	7	20	24
Sci-fi	8	11	28
Thriller	9	13	29
Travel	4	18	25
War	10	16	30

Plenary

Consolidating work on genre

Below are ten extracts from ten different genres. Using this material ask students to complete one of the activites that follow.

Genres

1. Mr Wallace sipped his cold coffee and stared out of the window at the rain splashing in the street. One thought troubled him. If they had got the right man why had he made that phone call? Mr Wallace had the overwhelming feeling that he hadn't quite got all the facts – yet!

2. McGee saw his chance and did not hesitate. He flung himself onto the body of the enemy tank and with superhuman effort prized open the hatch. He pointed his gun in and shouted: 'all of you out, now! – or I'll shoot. Move! Go, go, go!'

3. Peter rode his bike as fast as he could in the fading light. The lane suddenly dropped down a steep slope and he picked up valuable speed. He had an idea at the bottom of the hill. He got off his bike and hurriedly hid it under some bushes. Then he went to the other side of the lane where the bushes were even thicker. He buried himself in the undergrowth and kept perfectly still, hardly daring to breathe. Slowly a dark car approached and Peter could just see grim faces with rat-like eyes searching the sides of the lane.

4. Katie looked at her watch for the third time. Surely he hadn't forgotten. Another ten minutes went by and with welling annoyance she got up from the table and left the café. After a few paces she stopped in horror. There was her boyfriend, as large as life chatting and laughing with a lovely blonde young woman and pointing into a jeweller's window. She marched up to him.
   'What is going on?' she demanded angrily, her eyes flashing with emotion.
   'Hi Katie. What's the matter? This is my sister Helen. If you must know she's helping me choose your birthday present!'
   Katie looked at Nick and her eyes filled with tears.

5. Something woke her. The room was in deep shadow and she got out of bed and went across to the window. The lawn was bathed with the silver light of a full moon. She thought she saw something moving at the far edge of the lawn. She looked again. She must have been mistaken. There was nothing there. She turned from the window and was just about to return to bed when she caught a glimpse of her large mirror on the wall. In it she could see reflected the faint image of the garden and she could swear that there was a twisted shape moving smoothly across the grass towards the house.

6. I had travelled all night on the night train and had had the most uncomfortable journey of my life. The temperature was unbearably hot, we had run out of fresh water and the sleeping compartments were hideously overcrowded. Most of the night someone had been sitting in my head! I stepped off the train at our destination into the blazing light with a great sense of relief. I could think of only one thing. 'Water. Where could I get some water?'

7. Shane pushed open the swing doors to the bar and stepped in. The music, shouting and laughter all stopped and everyone looked round at the intruder.
    'I'm looking for Hank!' said Shane and swaggered in and up to the bar. 'Give me a shot of your best whiskey barman, while I wait.'
    'There ain't no Hank here,' said the barman and his eyes flickered nervously around the room.

8. Sujay ran in, hot bothered and late for the important interview. He slipped on the polished floor and collided with the tea trolley. A tray of cream cakes were deposited on his head. At that moment the manager came out of his room and was just about to say 'next please' when he caught a glimpse of Sujay who was trying to put what was left off the cakes onto the trolley and gave the young lady a weak smile.

9. There was a low hum which vibrated the floor and the doors slid closed behind her. Chloe looked up at a large screen.
    'Where are you taking me?' she asked in a trembling voice.
    'Back to our own galaxy. We have finished our work here!' replied a metallic voice.

10. As the candle flickered it became clear that his situation was grim. The trap door had been closed above him and he found himself in a sort of pit. Slithering on the floor around him were hundreds of snakes of various lengths and thicknesses. As he held the candle over them their heads raised up and turned towards him and he became aware of glassy sinister eyes holding him in a deathly stare.

Activities

🄴 Identify the genre

Ask students to identify the genre of each example.

🄼 Identify and explain

Ask students to identify the genre of each example and then write reasons for their choices.

🄲 Continue the extract

Ask students to choose one example and then to continue it in the appropriate style.

Starter

The narrator

Useful when the focus of the lesson is to look at narration.

Materials required: You will need several packs of playing cards (the larger the better); a few chess sets; a box containing a variety of miscellaneous objects.

Explain to the class that narration, at its basic level, is the telling, relating or recounting of something. To get the students straight into it you are going to use narration to bring alive various visual props. Divide the class into pairs (student A and student B). Provide them with a set of objects and a narrator sheet. A will act as narrator and B will display the objects.

For the three different levels, use the three different narrator sheets and the three different groups of objects detailed below. Allow the pairs time to rehearse their narration and then ask one pair from each group to present their narration to the whole class.

Teacher's tip

With all three levels explain to the students that the narrator, student A, must read and then provide appropriate pauses for the presenter, student B, to hold up the item at the appropriate time. The audiences' attention will be engaged visually by the item while they listen to the narration. Point out that there will be times in the narration when no objects will be presented and the audience just listen to the narrator. There will also be times when two objects are shown together to match the sense of the narration. Sometimes an object may need to be moved about. Tell them not to worry if they get it wrong as it is a fun experiment. Highlight the way the narration brings the objects alive and gives them meaning.

Activities

❺ The lover of flowers

Cards required: ace of hearts, ace of spades and the king of diamonds.

Give the three cards to student B and the narration sheet to student A, then ask them to rehearse the narration: 'The lover of flowers'.

The lover of flowers – narration sheet

(*Student B holds up the red ace*). 'There was once a man who could run so fast, that no one could beat him. Every year at the games he won. But there was a jealous man.' (*Student B now holds up the black ace.*) He wondered and wondered. 'I want to win' he thought. 'But how can I when he runs so fast?' One day the king summoned the jealous man. (*Student B now holds up the red and black ace*). 'Look at all these wonderful flowers that the fastest runner gathers for me from the forest. I would like you to gather me flowers also and bring them to me. The fastest runner loves flowers and if he sees nice ones he always stops to collect them for me. Now go!' (*Student B puts the cards down, then raises the black ace slowly*). The jealous man then has an idea. If the fastest runner loves flowers so much, in the next race I will put some very unusual ones by the side of the road and he will stop to pick them for the king and I shall win the race. And that is exactly what he did. He planted the most amazing and unusual flowers by the side of the track and sure enough (*student B holds up the red ace*) the fastest runner stopped to pick them. As they approached the finishing line the jealous man was ten centimetres in front of the fastest runner (*student B holds up the two aces to show the black ace just in front.*) Suddenly the fastest runner held out the flowers and the flowers passed the finishing line before the jealous man. The jealous man complained bitterly that it was unfair but the king (*student B holds up the king card*) was overjoyed with his flowers and pronounced that the fastest runner had won the race!

Ⓜ Nothing keeps me away from true love

Chess pieces required: king, knight, two castles (one white one black), queen.

Give student B the selected chess pieces and student A the narration sheet. Ask them to rehearse the narration: 'Nothing keeps me away from true love'. Explain that as the narrator reads his narration, student B is to hold up and move the appropriate piece at the appropriate time.

Nothing keeps me away from true love – narration sheet

'One day a brave knight, after miles of heavy riding, arrived at the king's castle. The king noticed that on his arm were tattooed the words: 'nothing keeps me away from true love'. The king then set a challenge. 'Look at my queen' he said. 'She is beautiful but I love another. I want to divorce her. Do you love her?' The knight, most surprised at this, gazed at the queen and immediately fell in love with her. 'I do love her', he said truthfully. 'Very well,' said the King. 'I will lock her in the great hall and place guards on the doors. Your challenge is to find a way in. If you do, I will divorce her and you may marry her. If you fail, you will spend the rest of your life in my dampest, darkest dungeon. Do you accept the challenge?' The knight accepted the challenge. The knight then constructed a miniature castle from the wood of the forest and adorned it with the berries and flowers of the hedgerows. He put it outside the great castle doors and hammered on them. He then hid himself inside. When the guards opened the doors they heard a voice from the miniature castle that said, in a disguised voice: 'I am the castle of wisdom. Ask any question and I shall answer it!' The guards carried the castle to the king, who bemused said: 'What is my biggest problem at the moment, oh wise castle?' In a strange voice the miniature castle said: 'you do not love your queen and seek a divorce!' Amazed, the king ordered that the castle be carried into the great hall where the queen was to ask the wise castle a question. When it was placed before her everyone was surprised to see the knight emerge and take the queen's hand, tenderly. With a smile he turned to the king. 'You see,' he said. 'nothing keeps me away from true love!' The king agreed on a divorce and the knight and queen lived happily ever after.

❻ What is the real value of things?

Range of objects required (for example): imitation jewels; a bottle of water; hotels from a monopoly game.

Give the students the objects and ask them to create their own short narrative where the objects become of enormous value.

Teacher's tip

It is really important to allow enough time for students to write their narratives and to present becuase they will love creating them and have fun doing them.

Plenary

Reflecting on narration

These exercises are designed to highlight and bring to life extracts of narration studied in the main part of the lesson. Ask students to work in small groups.

Activities

ⓔ Re-telling one small part

Split students into groups of three. Ask them to choose a small part of the story they have been looking at today and ask each one of them to read a different section of it.

Ⓜ Acting out the story with a narrator

Ask students to choose a small part of the story they have been looking at today and get them to act out the story, using three students to mime and a fourth to narrate what is happening as the students mime.

ⓖ Before and after narrator

Ask students to find a small part of the story they have been looking at today. Invite one of the students to be narrator and to prepare the audience by telling them the story so far. Then get the rest of the students in the group to act out the small scene using actions and voice, then to stand still while the narrator then explains what has just happened.

Teacher's tip

A presentation of examples of the students' work is very important here. It works well for the teacher to oversee the students as they work out their presentations and then the teacher can highlight small examples from each one to make a series of learning points. Discuss with the students how the narration controls how the audience think and feel about the action they see.

Starter

Setting, atmosphere and mood

Just right for when you want to prepare the students to think about setting, atmosphere and mood in prose fiction.

Materials required: a set of six different coloured highlighter pens for each group.

Explain to the class that the mood of a story can be created by a number of elements including weather, place, people, noises, objects and time. Divide the class into six mixed ability teams of five, nominate one student to be the leader, and explain that they are going to have a little competition between groups to create the most effective mood and atmosphere for various types of stories.

Give each group a 'Mood and atmosphere story setting sheet'. Tell them that as a group they have to pick the most suitable characteristics to set the mood for each different genre. A good way to do it is for the group to spend some time discussing and then highlight the story type and then with the same colour, highlight the six elements they have chosen for that genre. When the time is up ask the leader of each group to present their results. You should score on the chart points for appropriate choices. The scoring chart to display is available online.

Teacher's tips

- One of the key learning points and the part where attention can be held is when the teacher considers the presentation as the leader of the group gives feedback; the teacher should highlight and amplify examples with such expressions as: 'excellent – because…'

- It works extremely well if the teacher offers extra points for comments which the students may make when presenting their choices. An example of a suitable comments is shown online. Show this to the students to encourage them to make imaginative and creative comments.

Mood and atmosphere story setting sheet

Six types of story:

1. Fear and tension.

2. A peaceful and relaxing atmosphere.

3. A spooky feeling.

4. Cheerfulness and joy.

5. Love and affection.

6. A sad, thoughtful and mournful feel.

A. Weather conditions

1. Warm, but as the evening draws on the temperature turns cold and a grey drizzle of rain begins.

2. Early morning in spring with the sunshine bursting through the clouds.

3. Warm summer evening with golden sunshine.

4. Powerful gale force wind sending objects crashing down the street.

5. The sun was shining and a cool breeze gave soft and gentle relief.

6. Dark clouds were gathering and a distant rumble of thunder could be heard.

B. Place in which it is set

1. The castle was at the top of a steep crag of rock and the sheer drop to the sea and rocks below was breathtaking.

2. A ruin of a deserted hospital.

3. A huge garden with many trees, bushes and flowers bordered by an ancient wall.

4. An old cottage where everything has gone to rack and ruin.

5. The palm tree branches gently moved and beyond them stretched a beautiful white beach and then a deep blue sea with a silent white sail in the distance.

6. A village hall laid out with balloons, prepared party tables and smiling friendly DJ at the ready.

C. People involved

1. Out of the shadows a face appeared. It was a strange shape, more like a skull than a face and it was bathed in a faint and sickly yellow glow.

2. A group of people dressed in all kinds of fancy dress.

3. Someone hiding and someone in full pursuit.

4. A young boy who misses his deceased grandma.

5. A beautiful young woman and a handsome strong young man.

6. The man was dressed in shorts and plain T-shirt and was deeply calm and moved gracefully, like a cat, as if all tension had been taken from his body.

D. Noises in the background

1. The crashing of objects being flung about.

2. There were distant creaks and the dull sound of a step, then a leg being dragged and then a dull muffled moan.

3. The beautiful sound of birds nesting.

4. A young woman was singing quietly to the accompaniment of a gently strummed guitar.

5. Laughter, cheers and shouts and upbeat music.

6. A single violin playing an old nursery rhyme.

E. Primary objects in the story

1. There on the table was the photograph. It showed his grandma, when she was young, holding that doll. He picked up the actual doll which had been left to him. Even though it was now dusty and fragile he hugged it and couldn't let go of it.

2. Cakes, biscuits and every kind of sandwich.

3. Bits of old hospital equipment, like surgical knives, discarded, rusty and broken.

4. A small exquisite ring with a sparkling diamond.

5. There was an old antique chest made of ugly dark wood with a heavy lock. It looked like it hadn't been opened for many years.

6. A tall cool glass of orange juice with a blue straw, a slice of lemon and a small cocktail stick with a cherry.

F. Time frame

1. 11 o'clock in the morning, in mid summer, in the present day.
2. Set in the present day on a winter's afternoon as it starts to get dark.
3. It was pitch dark in the early hours of the morning in the middle of November, 100 years ago.
4. Early evening summertime in the present day.
5. Set today as dusk falls one autumn evening, but looking back to years before.
6. Set in the present day in early evening summer time.

Teacher's tip

The table below shows the match ups which work well, offered purely as a rough guide. Please note that many of the elements are interchangeable. A group may decide on other variations and gain extra points by being able to creatively explain their thinking clearly at score time. If you haven't got time for all the story types in the starter you may choose to do just one or two this time and some more another time. This will allow more time for the important comments.

Teacher's answers

Story type	Weather	Place	People	Noise	Objects	Time
Fear	4	2	3	1	1	2
Peaceful	5	5	6	4	6	1
Spooky	6	1	1	2	5	3
Cheerful	2	6	2	5	2	6
Love	3	3	5	3	4	4
Sad	1	4	4	6	1	5

Plenary

Fun with setting, atmosphere and mood

Provide students with a set of photos. Pictures that you could use are:

an old building; quiet lake scene; old quayside; Roman ruin; RNLI rescue boat in action; plate of healthy food; snowscape; birthday party table; stormy night scene; fashion shop; stained glass window; old cafe; old wall; chocolate shop window display; ice-cream kiosk sign; fallen oak tree; barbecue flames; a pier; a dog wearing silly glasses; a plane in the sky; sand dunes; an old fashioned bicycle; medieval fayre; carnival dancers; a child's toy; a full up skip.

Alternatively, a variety of pictures have been provided online for you to use in this plenary.

Divide students into small mixed ability groups and ask them to decide what sort of mood and atmosphere each picture might create. You can extend this activity by also asking them to outline ideas for a story that might be inspired by such a picture. The groups can jot down ideas as a group and then elect a spokesperson to feed back.

Teacher's tips

- It is a good idea to show one picture and then let all the groups work on that picture for a few minutes at the same time, and then feedback, one spokesperson at a time, while the picture is still shown to the class. It might not be practical to get feedback from every group for every picture, just make sure all the groups get a turn, by the time the plenary is finished.

- There is an example of comments which the students might make online. There can be read to the class to give them a stimulus of how a picture can inspire a particular mood and atmosphere. This may also give rise to ideas for what might happen in such a story. Remind the class that they do not have to be limited to the six types of story in the starter but may wish to broaden the scope.

Starter

Plot and story

Ideal when the main lesson is about studying plot, focusing on the order of events.

The aim of the task is for students to work out interesting suggestions for the plot of a story to focus their attention on the way events are organised. Tell students that in its basic form a plot is a plan of events in a prose fiction (or play or poem) organised in a way that will interest and engage the curiosity of the reader. Ask students to complete the relevant task below. Once the students have worked on their plot ideas ask some of them to present their ideas to the class.

> ### Teacher's tip
>
> For each task below, students are only required to give plot ideas, not to write the whole story.

Activities

ⓔ Alex's ambition

In pairs, (student A and B) ask students to read the opening of the story 'Alex's ambition' then to work together to come up with a suggestion of what might happen next in the story. If they need prompting, ask them: 'What might Alex do in an attempt to arrange a meeting with Peter?'

> ### Alex's ambition
>
> Alex wanted to be a professional footballer since the day his father took him, when he was only four years old, to the big match. Now that he was 13 he was captain of the school team and everyone marvelled at his skill with the ball.
>
> One day a famous footballer called Peter visited the school to give a talk about what it was like to be a professional footballer.
>
> Alex realised that he just had to arrange a meeting with Peter, somehow, as he felt strongly that Peter was just the right person who might be able to help him with that 'lucky break'.

Teacher's tips

- Online there are some prompt suggestions to use if the students have trouble coming up with an idea, for example: 'Maybe Alex could hang around until all the other students have gone and then approach Peter for a short chat'. Tell students that they could take one of these suggestions and develop it.

- When students present their ideas back to the class, tell student A to read the opening of the story and student B to explain what happens next.

Ⓜ The famous scientist

In pairs, (student A and B) ask students to read the end of the story 'The famous scientist' and to then come up with suggestions as to what events may have led to this ending. Say to them: 'The story of this scientist's great life had begun many years before. What do you think this scientist had achieved which had caused such importance in the world?'

The famous scientist

The famous scientist's condition had worsened over night and she lay there, the next morning, looking very poorly, with her family seated around her bed obviously worried. They thought about her long and eventful life. Piled up in the next room were literally thousands of get well messages sent from all parts of the world. Outside a large crowd had gathered and the world's press jostled for position. Some of the crowd held up boards with messages like: 'How can we ever thank you for what you have done?' lovingly scrawled on them.

Teacher's tips

- Ask students to suggest the type of things that the scientist may have done in order to be so highly regarded and famous. If they have trouble with ideas there are a range of prompt ideas on online, for example: 'Maybe she managed to develop a cure for a terrible disease.'

- Encourage the students to be imaginative. Perhaps the story could be set in the future. Develop their skill of asking the creative 'what if?' question. Remind them that the key thing with plot is to develop a set of events which interest and draw in the reader. For the presentation ask student A to suggest the events which led up to the ending and student B to read the ending to show how it links in.

● Monet's *Water Lilies*

Tell students to get into groups of three (students A, B and C) and to read the middle of the story 'Monet's *Water Lilies*'. In their group tell them to come up with what events could precede and follow the extract.

Monet's *Water Lilies*

The museum guard walked slowly round the art gallery, arms behind his back, and nodded and smiled at the customers. One particular customer, who to anyone watching, appeared to be a complete stranger, was not nodded at or smiled at. Instead, he was given a very discreet wink. Just then all the lights went out and there was the sound of surprised comments in the darkness. A few moments later and the lights were back on. The guard said 'Sorry about that everyone. I hope it didn't alarm you.' A few pleasant jokes were made and very soon everything returned to normal. The museum manager popped in to check that everything was OK. It appeared to be a mystery as to why the lights had suddenly gone out. The caretaker was asked to check the electrics.

At 5 o'clock the museum was closed in the normal way. The guard made his final round, as is procedure, and then let out a shout of alarm. The other staff came running to him. He pointed to the Monet *Water Lilies*. Someone had cleverly removed the original painting and had replaced it with a full sized print!

Teacher's tips

- When the three students present their ideas to the class it works well if student A explains the preceding plot idea and then student B reads the middle part of the story followed by student C giving the ideas for the plot which might follow on from the extract.

- There is a prompt idea online for the preceding and following events which you should read to students if they are struggling.

Plenary

Playing with the plot

Pick one of the activities below to finish a lesson that has been based on a work of fiction.

Activities
ⓔ Re-telling the main events of the story

Ask students to make some notes and then within one minute re-tell the main events of the story they have been studying.

> ### Teacher's tip
>
> It works well after hearing a couple of examples to ask the rest of the class if they agree with the choices of main events and if they would like to comment or add anything.

ⓜ Deciding which are the important events

This works well with a group of six students. Ask them to make some notes and select five events from the story. They are then to work out the importance of each event. Next, five students each adopt the pose of a statue which represents the events and arrange themselves in a line up in front of the class in their order of importance. The sixth student acts as narrator and dramatically explains what each statue represents and comments on its comparative importance.

> ### Teacher's tips
>
> • Remind the students that the order of the line is to represent the order of importance of the event, rather than the time order of the event. Online there is a worked example of how this may be done using part of a Shakespeare play as an illustration.
>
> • After this exercise ask the students to reassemble into the order as presented in the story and then invite each statue to say briefly, in turn, what event he represented and the class can see, in a very clear way, how the plot take shape as a whole.
>
> • It is always a good idea, to reinforce the main point about plot after this exercise has been done, to restate that it is the order of events in a plot which is so important as it is designed to engage and hold the interest of the audience.

ⓒ Deciding which are the important events: extended version

This task works well with groups of five students. Ask students to decide on the five most important events of the story, to pick one each, and then to stand at the front of the class to present their work, arranging themselves in order of importance. Each student then takes it in turn to act out, using a small space and in just ten seconds, the key points of their event. They can give a commentary, or narration on it themselves as they go along.

Teacher's tip

Once the presentations have been made, it is a good idea to ask for comments from the rest of the class. Online there is a worked example of how this activity may be done using part of a Shakespeare play as an illustration. It works well when the teacher shows a few possible ideas for acting out the events as this encourages the students to have a go. As mentioned in the previous Teacher's tip, it is good to re-enforce the importance of the order of events in a plot and asking the students to each act out their part in the order it occurs in the plot is useful.

Starter

Exploring theme

A great starter when you want to get the students looking at the theme of a piece of fiction.

Explain to the class that 'theme' in literature means the main idea of the work. Mention that a work can have more than one theme. Read the following story to the class.

The boy who wanted to juggle

Joshua, at the age of eight, visited the travelling circus and when he went home he decided that he wanted to be a juggler in a circus. His mother bought him some juggling balls and every day he practiced juggling. At first he kept dropping the balls but slowly he became better and better. When he went to high school he practiced juggling in the evenings and at weekends. He left school and got a job in a bank. He still juggled every evening. He got married and had children and every evening, without fail, he still practiced his juggling. He got to the stage where he could juggle nine balls in the air, a feat very few jugglers in the whole world could do. He kept it private and not many people knew about his juggling skills outside of his close family and friends.

One day, when he was 50 years old, he took his children to the circus. When it was time for 'The Great Julio, World Famous Juggler' Joshua got very excited. But the ringmaster stepped forward with a worried face and said: 'Ladies and Gentlemen. I am sorry to report that The Great Julio lies in bed with a high fever and we have therefore got to cancel the juggling performance tonight!' The sound of regret rippled around the audience and then the ringmaster added 'unless ... just a long shot I know but ... unless someone in the audience can juggle...' Joshua got up and stepped into the ring to the delight of his children, the applause of the crowd and the surprise of the ringmaster. 'I can juggle,' he said. After 42 years Joshua's moment had arrived!

Select the appropriate task from the list on the next page. When the students have completed the task ask a few of them to explain to the class what they have found.

Activities

❸ Identify the theme

Tell students to work in pairs. Ask them to try to work out what the main theme in the story is using the 'Some common themes in literature' work sheet below.

Some common themes in literature

Injustice	Good v evil	Overcoming difficulties	Guilt	Truth
Time changes things	Greed	Patience	Old age	Knowledge
Death	Power	Wealth	Beauty	Fear
Love	Justice	Temptation	Hope	Boredom
Reality and dreams	Loneliness	War	Honour	Success

ⓜ Highlighting the key quotes

Tell students to work in pairs to identify what the theme in the story is and then to highlight in the story the key quotes which directly indicate that theme.

❻ Are there any other themes?

Ask students to work in pairs to identify more than one possible theme that appears in the story and then to highlight in the story the key quotes which directly indicate those themes.

Plenary

Theme bingo

Use the worksheet from the starter 'Some common themes in literature' as the starting point for creating a theme bingo card. Use the same themes listed but create a variety of cards with the themes in different orders. Create enough different cards for every member of the class and give them one each.

Show the students the PowerPoint online which contains 15 short extracts of stories and get the students to highlight the theme on their chart that best represents the theme of the extract. Emphasise to them that they can only choose one. Tell students the first person to get a line and have their answers checked by you is the winner of theme bingo!

Example of an extract

'What is the matter Katie?' Sam had her arm around Katie and tried to comfort her.
'In a dream last night I fought with a horrible monster who was dressed in a huge pink coat with lime green buttons. I tore one of it's buttons off. I can see it so clearly,' sobbed Katie.
'Don't worry, it's only a horrible dream and its all gone now,' soothed Sam.
'But I just found this in my pocket!' cried Katie and held out a huge lime green button.

Answer: Dreams and reality

Teacher's tips

- Having 'correct' answers (provided online) gives the exercise focus and as a guide there is a best fit list below for quick assessment. However, the student may have chosen a different theme and be able to give a good explanation as to why. The ability to think about the larger picture of themes and main ideas is what this exercise is all about so it may well be possible to give points for well argued cases. For ease of reference ask students to jot the number of the extract against the theme on their chart.

- Note, students can choose more than one theme for an extract but they should only mark one off on the bingo sheet. It is good to get the students actively involved in reading out the extracts. You may wish to adapt by saying that any four in a row wins a prize as the bingo sheet is quite big.

Section 3
Reading fiction, poetry and drama

Starter

Exploring rhyme

Great for lessons when the focus is on the use of rhyme.

The appropriate activity can be selected from below where the exercise demonstrates, in an active and comparative way, the difference between ordinary prose and rhyme.

Activities

❺ Prose vs poetry

Ask students to work in pairs and give one of them a copy of the swimming instructor prose and one of them the poem. Tell them that one of them should read the prose to their partner and then the other should read the poem back to them. Tell them they are then to discuss the differences between the two and write a few sentences in answer the questions:

The two versions describe the same event.

- What does the rhyme add?

- Which version do you prefer and why?

The swimming instructor prose and poetry

The swimming instructor: prose
One day, it was hot and sunny and, having nothing to do but walk the streets, I decided to go to the beach. I noticed a crowd of people gathered round someone who was standing next to a huge inflatable mini swimming pool. He was a swimming instructor and he was giving free lessons for people who could not swim. Nearby was an ice cream kiosk and ice creams were handed out for free. Next to that was a pretty cart loaded with all sorts of sweets and a sign which read 'Help yourself'. I had such fun there – I stayed all day and learnt how to swim. Quite a few of my friends had turned up and had a great time larking about and eating as much ice cream and sweets as they wanted. It occupied my mind all day but at the back of my mind was a deep longing for you. I wished you had been there with me.

The swimming instructor: poem
I went to the warm sunny beach,
And saw something really quite cool;
A swimming instructor would teach,
Anyone how to swim in the pool.

And the ice creams were free for that day,
With a 'help yourself' sign by the sweets,
There really was nothing to pay,
In this way we were kept off the streets.

And I had fun until it was dark,
And became a good swimmer too,
My friends all had such a great lark,
But I wished I had been there with you!

Ⓜ Fish and chips mini plays

Ask students to work in groups of three and act out the two versions of the mini plays 'fish and chips'. Tell them that once they have practiced they will be asked to present their mini plays to the class and suggest what the rhyme does to change things.

Fish and chips mini plays

These two versions of the mini plays involve three characters:

A = student, B= student's friend, C= man serving fish and chips.

Fish and chips: prose

A: Could I have a large cod and chips please?

B: And could I have a large sausage and chips please?

C: Certainly. Would you like them open or wrapped?

A: Open please.

C: Yours open too?

B: Yes please.

C: That will be three pounds and fifty pence please. Thank you. A five pound note so that's one fifty change. There we go. Would you like salt and vinegar on those?

A: Yes please. Lots of vinegar please.

B: No vinegar on mine and just a little salt, thanks.

C: There we are.

A: Thank you.

B: Thank you.

C: Please call again.

A: We will, it's good here!

Fish and chips: rhyming version

A: Could I have cod and chips please to keep my hunger at bay?

B: And I'd like chips with sausages to help me on my way.

C: Certainly, I will get them, I will fish them from the fryer.

When you've eaten these you'll find your energy much higher.

A: I want to eat them straight away, so please don't wrap mine up,

B: Could mine be open also, as they're easier to sup?

C: Would you like some salt and vinegar to add a bit of flavour?

A: Yes, I think that would be nice and the taste I'd really savour!

C: That will be three pounds and fifty to pay for all your meal.

B: Here's a five pound note, I think it quite a bargain deal!

C: Here's your change – one fifty, and please call back some time.

A: Certainly, we'll call again as your service is so fine.

Teacher's tip

Point out to the students that in ordinary prose our attention is not on the words themselves but just on the things the words are talking about. In the rhyming version we tend to think about the way things are said rather than just what is said. The sound and rhythm of the words becomes interesting in themselves.

ⓒ *A Bar at the Folies-Bergère* by Édouard Manet

Ask the students to work in pairs and start by looking at a copy of the painting of *A Bar at the Folies-Bergère* by the artist Édouard Manet (widely available on the internet). They are then to read the prose description and the poem version below and write down a few notes to answer the questions on the next page.

- Which version is most interesting and why?

- What does the rhyme add to the meaning?

A Bar at the Folies-Bergère by Édouard Manet

A Bar at the Folies-Bergère by Édouard Manet: prose

I'm standing in the art gallery looking at the wonderful painting called *A Bar at the Folies-Bergère*, by the artist Édouard Manet. There is a sweet young woman in the centre of the picture, looking into the distance beyond us. Behind her is a large mirror reflecting the crowds of people in the bar. I can imagine that if I was there the noise of the talking and possibly music would be very loud. She is wearing a pretty charm around her neck with some nice pink flowers below it. It has the feeling and atmosphere of late at night and yet she stands so calm and peaceful. On the bar in front of her is a bowl of oranges and groups of neatly arranged bottles. A thought occurs to me as I look at her. I wonder if she ever had children and if so, after all this time, I wonder what those children's, children's children are doing now. The style of painting is interesting. Manet seems to deliberately blur the images in places. He uses wonderful colours. Then I have quite a thought. If he hadn't painted this picture I would have had no knowledge and no idea of the existence of this woman at all. Quite a thought really. It is only the painting that allows me to know anything about her existence!

A Bar at the Folies-Bergère by Édouard Manet: poem

I do not know her name, the woman at the bar,
Looking so beautifully sweet, with eyes staring afar;
That mirror at the back, reflecting a vast crowd –
I wasn't ever there, of course, but I bet it was quite loud!
Round her neck, a pretty charm and below, a pink flower,
Her mood is so very calm, for such a very late hour.
The oranges look sweet with bottles grouped around,
I wonder after all these years, if she has descendants to be found?
The artist had such great skill, look at the chandelier blurred-
The colours used give such a thrill, but I am quite disturbed,
To think that it's only paint, that brings these visions here alive,
Without the artist's work, nothing of her would survive!

Plenary

The rhyme quiz

Split the class into four teams and display a score board on the flipchart. Tell them they are going to compete against each other in the rhyming quiz. Display the following quiz on a PowerPoint (available online) and read each slide aloud. For each slide ask students to put their hands up and guess words that fit the rhyming pattern specified as well as the sense of the poem. Award students points for correct answers on the scoreboard. Suggested answers are provided online.

The rhyme quiz

Round 1

(Rhyming scheme: aa)

The wonderful painting on the _____

Makes her look pretty, young and _____

Round 2

(Rhyming scheme: aa, bb)

I have travelled to countries far and _____

Setting sail on the sea at high _____.

To many lovely places I have _____

And countless wonders I have _____.

Round 3

(Rhyming scheme: ab, ab,)

The bird soared high in the empty _____

As the grey sea raged even _____.

I've never seen my own _____

A more skilful _____.

Round 4

(Rhyming scheme: aaa)

Save your money when you _____

It doesn't matter if you're woman or _____

And one day you'll be grateful for the _____.

Round 5

(Rhyming scheme: aa, bb)

All day long I've used my _____

Each time I've been rung I heard the same _____.

When I write and receive a _____

There is no noise so I think it is _____

Round 6

(Rhyming scheme: ab, ab)

I buy new clothes to impress my _____

But get new ideas for _____.

Keeping others impressed will never _____

But a quiet full mind is great _____.

Round 7

(Rhyming scheme: ab, ab)

He saved his dog from the raging _____

And the dog it is quite _____.

But the brave man drowned, yes drowned did _____

And the story's too sad to _____.

Round 8

(Rhyming scheme: abccba)

I've been watching football since I was in my _____;

I follow my team wherever they _____.

And shout out my _____.

And then I _____

To plan the next visit, wherever they _____.

Yes, football is my life and keeps me _____!

Round 9

(Rhyming scheme: ababb)

Her song was better than I can _____

A wonderful voice and _____.

A lot of money I would _____,

To have that music _____.

It really is _____!

Teacher's tip

Students may well come up with rhyming words which are not on the suggested answer slide but if they fit and make sense then award them the points. Some rhymes are harder to solve than others so award points accordingly. There is a note of the rhyme scheme at the head of each slide to help guide the answers.

Starter

Pictures in the mind: imagery

Just right for when the lesson is planned to explore the way imagery works.

Materials required: drawing paper; coloured pencils; flipchart and coloured pens.

Explain to the class that 'imagery' usually means a visual picture although it can also refer to actions, feelings, thoughts and ideas and can appeal to some of or all of the senses. The main thing to remember is that the careful use of language allows us to imagine something in our mind. Usually a good image provides a clue and the imagination is able to add things to it to create a full 'picture'.

Ask the class to work in groups of three; this activity works well with mixed ability groups. The teacher reads aloud one of the extracts (nine rounds worth of extracts are listed below). One student from each group quickly sketches out an idea on paper in pencil which represents the overview of the image. They then pass the sheet to the next student who imaginatively adds colour to the drawing and then passes this to the third student in the group who adds some key words and phrases from the extract.

Tell the students they have 45 seconds to complete each stage. When the time is up, get the groups to hold up their finished work. The teacher nominates one of the groups to come to the front and copy (and improve) what they have done on to the flipchart to show the whole class. Encourage the students to comment on why they have chosen certain visual images to match the words, as they draw them.

Teacher's tips

- Online there is a PowerPoint including two worked examples which can be used to exemplify to the class the different stages of the activity step by step. Show the examples before the rounds begin. Stress to the students that the point of the exercise is not necessarily to be a great artist, the main thing is to explore the image by using the different ideas of different group members. For example, one student might get an idea for the first image and then another image idea may occur to the next student and so on. The group can decide who does which job, and they can switch round for later rounds.

- The timing is important here: 45 seconds for each task works quite well. The students will be keen to have another go and the 'reward' where they get to write it out on the flipchart makes most students eager to do a good job. As they copy their work onto the flipchart it is a good idea to read out the extract again so that the whole class can see the pictures become combined with the words.

Pictures in the mind: imagery

Round 1

Explain that this is a very short extract from a poem about war.

The Soldier's Medal

A soldier's gun lies there,

Half buried in the mud;

The soldier's medal daggles –

From the tree of blood.

Round 2

Sometimes sailors at sea feel very alone in the huge expanse of the ocean, especially at night. Here is a small glimpse of a sailor's experience.

No Light at All

The grey sea stretches to the furthest point,

The moon seems strangely small;

The waves heave like a sleeping beast

And the stars have no light at all.

Round 3

Sometimes poets get you to think by using images which don't seem to go together. This creates mystery.

The Snail

Have you ever stopped to see a snail,

In very early morn?

Have you ever seen your loved one –

Look at you and yawn?

Have you found a love letter –

Lying newly torn?

Round 4

Sometimes images are suggested by general images about well known things.

The Greatest Theme Park

For years and years we waited –

And now we're here at last!

The Greatest Theme Park on the Earth –

Where rides go incredibly fast!

Round 5

Sometimes the images capture a moment in time. This extract from a poem describes a group of traditional gypsies, in the 19th century, camping down in the countryside after a day's travelling.

Among the wild flowers

Somewhere in the perfumed meadows,

Somewhere near the murmuring brook,

Seated round the evening fire

Unshaven faces wearily look

Into the flames that sooth the mind,

Among the wild flowers of every kind.

Round 6

Sometimes images are surreal and full of fantasy. This poem describes an apple taking a holiday.

Why shouldn't an apple?

Why shouldn't an apple go on holiday – and lay upon the beach?

Why shouldn't an apple have ice cream and cola within its reach?

Why shouldn't an apple get a suntan and wear sunglasses too?

Why shouldn't an apple have a holiday, and be just like you?

Round 7

Sometimes the poem's images ask questions about the future.

What will it be like?

What will it be like, in centuries on from here?

Will people still be drinking water, tea and beer?

Will people travel round by still walking on their feet?

Will town centres be untidy or will they still be neat?

Will wars still be going on with fighting in the sky?

Will babies still be being born and feel the need to cry?

Round 8

Some poems deal with the images of friendship.

A good friend should

A good friend should always be there whatever happens in life,

You should be able to call on her when you're in the midst of strife.

A friend should feel good to be with, not putting you on edge,

A friend should be trustworthy, without a written pledge.

Yes, a friend should be with you at your rise and at your fall,

The passing of all the years should make no difference at all.

Round 9

How about a poem about teachers?

Teachers

What makes a good teacher?

It is quite hard to say,

Some teachers feel it's good and right

To shout at you all day!

Some teachers talk so boringly

They wonder why we yawn,

Some teachers work far too hard

And let their nerves be torn.

But sometimes, if you're lucky,

You will meet a teacher like mine,

Who smiles and cares and thinks a lot

And teaches me just fine!

Plenary

Image response form

Ask students to fill in the 'Image response form' based on an image found in the texts they have been studying in the main part of the lesson.

Image response form

Name of student_____
Copy the words of the image in this space:
Did you find it in a poem, a piece of prose or a play ? _____

Which of the senses did it appeal to and how strongly?	Could you do a lightning pencil sketch in this space to capture the essence of the image?	How much did you like the image?

Sense	Strong	Medium	Weak
Sight			
Sound			
Feel			
Taste			
Smell			

Tick the box ✓

High
Medium
Low

When you read and think about the image what else comes to mind? Use free writing and just let your ideas flow out...

Discuss with your partner what you thought about the image and find out what your partner thought. Jot down a few key point notes in this box:	Other thoughts...

Teacher's tip

Students usually like filling in forms. An important part of this exercise is to get them to reflect on an image carefully, slowly and without rush or hurry. It works well if they work in pairs and reflect on a different image each.

Starter

Similes work so well

Ideal for when the lesson is focussing on reading and understanding the use of similes in prose and poetry, and when the students are required to write and use similes.

What is a simile? Explain to the class that if you want to describe something which only you can see, you may want to compare it to something which everyone is familiar with, so that your reader can understand more clearly what you mean. For example, we might say someone is 'as busy as a bee'. It also makes the writing fun and interesting.

Select from the appropriate task below.

Activities

ⓔ Match ups

Ask students to match up the first part of the simile in section 1 with the second part in section 2.

Section 1

1. The foamy waves crashed against the rocks and looked like …

2. The wind lifted her hair like …

3. The ship far out to sea in the storm bobbed about like …

4. Rain had fallen all night and your feet on the grass sounded like …

5. I peered into the mouth of the erupting volcano and it seemed like …

6. The fisherman's beard was entangled like …

7. In the thunderstorm the huge chalk cliff was lit up for a split second and looked like …

8. The tree was bent over like …

Section 2

1. ... a cork in a bath tub.

2. ... huge snails being pulled off of the slimy sticky mud.

3. ... cream soda poured into a glass.

4. ... an old fishing net.

5. ... a ghost's pale face.

6. ... an old gypsy, twisted with age.

7. ... invisible giant's fingers.

8. ... a giant saucepan of jam bubbling.

Teacher's tip

Students who finish with time to spare could have a go at writing their own ideas for the second part of the simile. Encourage them to experiment and have fun. Suggest that a good starting place is to ask the question 'Now, what else can you think of which looks a bit like that?'

Ⓜ Enhancing a description using similes

Ask students to describe an old lonely castle using as many similes as they can. A suggested starting point of the description is given below for them to continue. Also, a set of suggestions are provided to help prompt their ideas.

An old lonely castle

Possible starting point:

'Thick ivy clung in clusters to the castle walls like frozen green bees on a hive ...'

Some suggestions to help prompt ideas:

1. Old dark arch shaped doorways where doors once stood reminded me of ...

2. The rugged edges of the castle walls, in the mist, could have been ...

3. Strange sounds came from the depth of the castle as if ...

Teacher's tip

Project a picture of an old castle onto the screen while the students work. Remind them to be careful not to make every sentence a simile but just to include a few well chosen ones. Encourage them to be adventurous and highly imaginative with their comparisons. Draw their attention to the examples shown above where there are variations on the basic 'like' or 'as' comparison formats.

© Evaluating similes

Ask students to read through the extract below and identify the similes. They are then to write 'evaluations' of the similes, expressing how effective they think they are. If they want to they can experiment with writing improvements to the similes. Two examples of an evaluation are given.

Evaluating similes

The Professor, who was dressed like a scarecrow, led his visitors into the front room as if they were geese. He proposed to show them his wonderful invention. In his excitement his arms waved about like the tentacles of a sea monster. He led the way along the narrow dim corridor, swaying his lantern to and fro, and dark shadows moved on the wall like giant insects.

He slowly opened the door to the laboratory. The small group of people cautiously stepped inside. There it stood. The world's first 'age removing machine'. It looked like an old fashioned phone booth. You simply sat in the special chamber, for three minutes and the appearance of three years of aging would be removed from your face! Four minutes would remove four years and so on up to a maximum of 30. He asked who wanted to try it first. One of the group stepped forward like a curious cat, inspecting the strange machine. Inside were many dials and switches and wires. The wires hung out from the controls like thin worms.

Evaluation 1: '…dressed like a scarecrow' is not that effective as it has become a cliché. Perhaps a better simile would be …

Evaluation 2: 'Dark shadows moved on the wall like giant insects.' This is an effective simile because I can picture the strange shapes of moving insects and they create quite a foreboding atmosphere.

Plenary

Reflecting on similes

Select the appropriate task from below.

Activities

🅔 Identifying similes

Find three similes in the work you have read today. Copy them out.

🅜 Re-using similes

Find three similes in the work you have read today. Copy them out. Write a short piece of original writing which re-uses those similes in a creative way.

🅖 Evaluating similes

Find three similes you have read and discovered in the text which you have looked at in today's lesson. For each one copy it out and comment on its effectiveness. If it works well try to be detailed in your comments about it.

Teacher's tips

It is a good idea to have a chart on the wall and display work created in this plenary to refer back to the next time you look at similes. Have three columns headed:

1. Examples of similes

2. Re-using similes

3. Evaluating similes

A small amount of time invested in a simple wall display yields great rewards when you refer back to them at a later point. It also raises the status of the students' work – they see it being used as a teaching. New examples can be added in future lessons.

Starter

The power of metaphor

Ideal when the lesson is focussing on reading and understanding the use of metaphors in prose and poetry, and for when students are required to write using metaphors.

What is a metaphor? Explain to the class that a metaphor is a use of language when one thing is described as if it was something else. It is like a simile but a simile is an 'explicit' comparison: e.g. 'the flower <u>was like</u> a heart', whereas the metaphor is an 'implicit' comparison: e.g. 'the flower <u>was</u> a heart.' A good anchor point is to think of the literal meaning and the metaphorical meaning. 'The footballer hammered the ball into the back of the net' makes us reflect that he didn't <u>literally</u> use a hammer. Motivate the interest of the class by telling them that good use of metaphor makes language sparkle and enriches interest.

Choose the appropriate activity from below.

Activities

❷ Match ups

Ask students to match up the metaphor in section 1 with the situations they describe in section 2.

Section 1

1	The mountainous pink ham steamed alongside the rivers of sauces and little further along snuggled a forest of broccoli.
2	In the doorway a ghost hovered, half pale, half shadow, in the silvery moonlight.
3	The sun shown in full glorious summer from her smiling face.
4	He piled the bricks of cash into his leather bag.
5	The night city wore a dress of sparkling diamonds and sapphires.
6	The face, for just a moment, was made of hard red marble with veins of purple.
7	The bullet of a fish sliced through the murky depths.

8	He looked down from the top of the gigantic redwood tree and noticed the small plastic figures from a toy shop looking up at him.
9	The cat's eyes were tiny yellow alien planets bathed in yellow tinted atmosphere.
10	The square shaped pizza was a Jackson Pollock painting, newly made.

Section 2

1	A woman's warm smile.
2	The pizza, with all sorts of mushrooms, cheese, chicken and tomatoes arranged in a random pattern was dished up hot.
3	The cat's eyes.
4	A man stood in the shadows in the moonlight.
5	He climbed the high tree and the people looked very small down below.
6	A fish swims quickly.
7	An angry face stares motionless.
8	A table loaded with food ready for a great feast.
9	A city at night with the lights on.
10	He put large quantities of cash into his bag.

Teacher's tips

- If students finish with time to spare ask them to try to write some metaphors for everyday things.

- As with the similes suggest that a good starting point is to find an everyday object and ask the question 'What does this look like?' and then try to write a metaphor.

Ⓜ Enhancing a description using metaphors

Ask students to write about a holiday (real or imaginary) using metaphors to enhance the writing. There is a suggested starting point below that students can continue. It also includes details to give students ideas for their metaphors.

Writing about holidays

'It was a great holiday. We toured so many places. A few places really stand out in my mind. Victoria Falls, for example, on the Zambezi River in Zambia was an impressive sight. The crashing of the frothy torrents was the sound of a monster playing a strange unknown musical instrument whose sounds, from deep below, got deep into the soul. I shall never forget the power of that sound. Egypt was amazing too. The gigantic statues of Pharaoh Ramses 11 stood there, after all this time, in the blazing sunshine. They were brooding monks, meditating, their minds lost in mystic wanderings, staring down at me with stone eyes …

Teacher's tip

Use pictures cut out from magazines of holiday destinations to prompt writing ideas. (Note: They have more perceived value to the students if they are cut carefully and presented on cards rather than straight from the magazine.) As with similes, remind students not to use too many metaphors but rather include a few well chosen ones. A great way to motivate work for this one is to get the student to visualise their ideal holiday and use that to write about. Give them a 'one minute visualisation' where you help the idea along by playing some holiday music and speak to them to create images of nice places.

Ⓒ Evaluating metaphors

Ask the students to read through the extract below and identify the metaphors. They are then to write 'evaluations' of the metaphors, expressing how effective they think they are. Two examples of an evaluation are given.

The summer morning walk

I love summer morning walks, don't you? Say you're on holiday and you don't have to worry about the rat race for a while. You can take your time, can't you? You can notice things, little details that you'd normally miss. Like a wasp I noticed eating the sugar from a discarded doughnut. Her little legs splayed out and she became, just for a moment, a miniature yellow and black trampoline.

I love, on such mornings, to stop and gaze at shop windows. There was a new shop I came across, which sold cheap scientific experiment kits for kids, and the arrangement of the kits' contents in the window was a frozen firework display of colours and shapes.

I sat at a café, outside of course, and waited for someone to clear the table. I noticed that a cup, half full of cold tea, was a cup half full of toffee. Eventually, when the table was cleared and my milkshake brought along to me, I was able to sink back and gaze lazily at the clouds. In those clouds dragons from ancient caves appeared and then changed to twisted faces of witches and then to laughing children. I closed my eyes and felt the comforting warmth of a 'nothing-to-do-ness' starting to shroud me in soft, warm candyfloss.

Walking from the café, and blinking in the increasing sunlight I saw that a drain lid had been lifted and I glanced down into the depths and heard the distressed captive voice of the dark whirling waters crying for freedom and sunshine.

Evaluation 1: 'rat race' is not that effective because it is over used.

Evaluation 2: '... she became a miniature yellow and black trampoline.' Is an effective metaphor because it makes an usual comparison and gets us to think carefully which helps us understand, in an interesting way, what the wasp looked like. It also, perhaps, gets us to think about the wasp in a new way. It therefore both interests and also entertains the reader.

Plenary

Reflecting on metaphor

Select the appropriate exercise to be applied to the work which was studied in the main part of the lesson today.

Activities

Ⓔ Identify the metaphors

Find three metaphors that you have read today. Copy them out.

Ⓜ Re-using metaphors

Find three metaphors in the work you have read today. Copy them out. Write a short piece of original writing which re-uses these metaphors in a creative way.

Ⓒ Evaluating metaphors

Find three metaphors in the work you have read today. For each one copy it out and comment on its effectiveness. Try to be detailed in your comments about it.

Teacher's tips

- Have a quick-fire feedback session for this plenary where you share their findings on the board and jot their comments down in note form. The teacher's comments, as the students ideas are jotted on the board, are very important here as they can confirm and share learning outcomes. A good way to finish off is to write three popular metaphors from the lesson's work, on the board, and have a class vote as to which one they liked best.

- As in the simile idea, it is also great to spend some time on a wall display to show the students' work in future lessons.

Starter

Exploring dialogue

Perfect for lessons that focus on the use of dialogue in literature. Considers how dialogue brings characters to life.

Materials required: you will need to display a copy of the painting of Van Gogh's *Bedroom in Arles* (widely available on the internet).

Explain to the students that dialogue is the speech of the characters and that it helps to bring the characters within the fiction to life. Tell students that the idea of the activity is to dramatically read out a scene from fiction in two ways, firstly with just narration and secondly with narration and dialogue. The class are then to compare the results and make some discoveries about the use of dialogue.

Read the following extract using just narration while the class look at the picture.

Extract A: narration

Vincent invited Paul into his bedroom and they sat down to talk. Vincent asked Paul if he wanted a glass of water and thanked him for travelling so far to see him. He went on to say how lonely he was and how glad he was to see him. Paul responded that he was pleased to be with him. Paul drank the water and looked round the small room. He felt sorry for Vincent because he seemed to have so little. Paul asked about the paintings on the wall and Vincent explained that they were recent ones he had done. When Paul went over to one and touched the surface, he mentioned that the paint seemed to be thrown onto the surface and asked whether Vincent was angry when he painted them. Vincent said that he had been passionate rather than angry. The two men looked at each other. Vincent was getting excitable whereas Paul was staying very calm. He asked Vincent if he liked painting and Vincent replied that it was his whole life and stated that he couldn't do anything else. The two men looked at each other again and Paul started to feel uneasy, as if he was beginning to think that Vincent was a little mad. Paul then asked Vincent what he had been doing in the storm the night before. Vincent stared at the wall and so Paul repeated the question. Vincent, after a long pause said that he had been painting and Paul said that it was mad to go out in that and asked him why. Vincent stared at the wall again and then said something about wanting to express the truth in paint and show the power of nature. Paul asked where the painting was and after another pause Vincent started to get upset and explained that the wind had blown the painting away. Paul started to look even more alarmed. He felt sorry for him and to help suggested that he rested more to which Vincent responded that if he stopped working it would be like stopping living. Paul asked how many pictures he had sold so far and the answer was sad. He had actually sold only one, to his brother, for only twenty francs. Paul felt even sorrier for him but also worried about Vincent's state of mind. To be helpful Paul asked if it wouldn't be better off to just get an ordinary job but Vincent turned on him in a state of high emotional distress and declared that one day people would really see the value of his work. He indicated that he had driven himself to the edge with it all but mumbled that it would be all right in the end. He sank his head in his hands and started crying. Paul, really alarmed by now, slowly edged out of the door.

Ask for three volunteers to dramatically read out the next example containing dialogue.

Extract B: narration and dialogue

Characters: A: Narrator; B: Vincent Van Gogh; C: Paul Gauguin, his friend.

A: Vincent invited Paul into his bedroom and they sat down to talk.

B: Would you like a glass of water, my dear friend? Thank you for travelling so far to see me. I'm so glad you're here, I get so lonely.

C: It's good to be here.

A: Paul drank the water and looked round the small room. He felt sorry for Vincent because he seemed to have so little.

C: What are those paintings on the wall? Did you do them?

B: Yes, they are some recent paintings I did.

A: Paul went over to one and touched the surface.

C: This paint seems to be literally thrown onto the canvas! Were you angry when you did them?

B: Not angry, just passionate about what I was trying to do!

A: The two men looked at each other. Vincent was getting excitable whereas Paul was staying very calm.

C: Do you like painting Vincent?

B: Like it? Painting is my whole life. I couldn't do anything else.

A: The two men looked at each other and Paul starts to feel uneasy, as if he begins to think that Vincent is a little mad.

C: You went out in that terrible storm last night until late into the night. What were you doing until then?

A: Vincent stares at the wall.

C: Vincent, what were you doing in the storm?

B: Painting.

C: But it was mad to go out in that. Why did you paint in such a storm?

A: Again Vincent stares at the wall.

B: Because I want to express the truth in paint about the power of nature.

C: Where is the painting you did? I'd like to see it.

B: You can't see it!

C: Why not?

A: Vincent starts to get upset.

B: Because the wind blew it away into the river.

A: Paul starts to look even more alarmed now.

C: You've got to start resting more Vincent. You're working too hard.

B: If I stop working, I stop living.

C: How many pictures have you sold so far?

B: One. To my brother Theo. For twenty francs.

A: Paul looks at Vincent in pity.

C: Is it worth all the trouble Vincent? Couldn't you just get an ordinary job?

A: Vincent turns to look at Paul and with great passion speaks.

B: One day Paul, one day, people will see what my art is really worth. It is driving me to the edge of my life but it will turn out all right in the end. It will turn out all right.

A: Vincent sinks his head into his hands and starts sobbing and Paul slowly backs out of the door.

Select the appropriate task from below.

Activities

❸ One difference

Ask students to write a sentence to identify one difference between the experience of listening to Extract A compared with Extract B.

Ⓜ Advantages and Disadvantages

Ask students to write a few sentences about the advantages and disadvantage of narration compared to narration and dialogue.

Ⓒ A short presentation

Ask students to prepare a short presentation, which could be presented to the rest of the class, to explain clearly the difference between narration and dialogue.

Plenary

Using dialogue

Select the appropriate task from the list below.

Activities

Ⓔ Narrating – what I did today

Ask students to write a small piece of narration recounting what they have done so far today.

Ⓜ Narrating and using dialogue – what I did today

Ask students to write a small piece of narration and dialogue recounting what they have done so far today.

Ⓒ Dialogue only – what I did today

Ask students to write a small piece of dialogue only recounting what they have done so far today.

Teacher's tip

Ask students to read to the rest of the class a few examples of what they have written and encourage a conversation about the use of dialogue.

Starter

Using stagecraft

Just right to prepare for lessons when stagecraft (preparing and designing the fiction for a dramatic presentation in the form of a play or role play), is used as a tool for exploring and understanding a work of fiction.

Read and show the students the sample extract below from a piece of fiction. Tell them that they are going to imagine that they have been given the job of director/producer and their task is to make brief notes using the 'Stagecraft brief ideas form' provided on the next page to 'stage' the scene in a dramatic way.

Adam and Jessica

The moment had arrived at last. Jessica, wearing her new outfit and feeling very uncomfortable, stood in a lounge of a top London Hotel waiting for Adam to walk through the door. She glanced again at her watch. One minute to go. Her heart beat furiously.

Adam and Jessica had been childhood sweethearts but five years ago, when they both left school, to her great astonishment, Jessica received no contact at all from Adam. He had become very successful in a pop band called Motion Men and although Jessica had cut out every article she could find about him in magazines and newspapers and stuck them in a scrapbook she had, and watched his progress on TV, she had received no communication from him whatsoever.

That was until yesterday. Yesterday she received a mysterious 'special delivery' letter from Adam summoning her to a very posh hotel in London. There she stood, waiting in the Grenadier Suite. The letter had specified the Grenadier Suite. What was all this about?

Unknown to Jessica, Adam, despite appearances, had been a very unhappy man these last few years. He had been involved in many shallow relationships but his feelings had developed into an intense rekindling of love for Jessica and, at the same time, a painful regret for ignoring her all these years. His intention was to meet her, apologise deeply for ignoring her and then to declare his love for her.

Stagecraft brief ideas form

Brief summary of scene to be staged.
Ideas for set design. (Would you have a detailed realistic set or a minimal bare stage?)
Lighting effects. (Consider colours, brightness, fades and colour mixes.)
Sound effects. (Which sounds effects would you use? How about music?)
Costumes. (Would these be natural or symbolic?)
Which actors would you use and what style of acting would you want? (Realistic or stylised e.g. slow motion?)
Props.
Other considerations.

Teacher's tips

- It is a good idea, when the students have had enough time to put down their notes on the form, to have a blank form projected on the board and for you to jot down ideas under the various headings as you pick out the best ideas from students' work.

- A good way to focus the work and create a sense of excitement is to repeat ideas back to the whole class as you jot them on the board. For example 'That's a great idea Simon, a low drum beat which gets louder as Adam walks in the room. That's a great way to build excitement … Maddie I'm going to pop your idea about the dress she's wearing on the board. I love the way her plain clothes will contrast with his extravagant ones and show the difference in their lifestyles … well done!' This sort of lively and active language in the feedback of the starter usually results in much more satisfying outcomes as students are keen to jot down even more ideas on their own forms in response to what goes up on the board.

- An important thing to remember is the quality of your comments at this stage. Acknowledge what they have done and then add comments which help teach, in a less direct way, the objectives of the starter.

- There is an example of a completed stagecraft ideas form online for your reference.

Plenary

Reflecting on stagecraft

Ask students to select scenes from the work they have been studying in the main part of the lesson and then ask them to fill out the 'stagecraft brief ideas form' from the linked starting based on these scenes.

You can either get students to complete their forms on their own and do a feedback session with the whole class as described in the starter, or another way to organise this activity is to get students to work in small groups on the stagecraft forms. Then each group can stand at the front and present their ideas to the class. This works really well if each group covers a different scene as it keeps the feedback more varied and interesting.

Teacher's tips

- Overseeing feedback is of vital importance. Supposing a group explain their ideas about lighting, in practice a lack of 'emphasis' can allow lots of great ideas to slip through almost unnoticed. It is your job, during the feedback session, to pause the process, draw attention to the point being made, and amplify its teaching potential, by making comments like 'Did you all catch that? Isn't that a great idea? The soft pink lighting grows stronger as the two approach each other! What a subtle effect that would be. We would emotionally feel their love, wouldn't we? Well done!'

- If students struggle, show them an example of a completed form based on a scene studied in the lesson. This will help to enhance and encourage their own ideas. The feedback of the plenary is important here to draw together ideas from the class. Jotting them up on the blank form on the board, as suggested in the starter, works very well here too.

- Another great way to start this activity to grab the interest of the class is to show them a completed stagecraft ideas form, instigate a whole class discussion about what the scene might look like and then show them a video of the scene the form was based on. This takes a lot of preparation from you, but it really brings the notes and the whole focus of stagecraft together in a dynamic way.

Section 4
Reading and writing: non-fiction

Starter

Summary skills and note taking

Perfect for when the lesson deals with how to take good notes and write summaries.

Explain to students that when they read a text it is of vital importance to their learning that they can take notes of the important parts and write clear and concise summaries. But how do we know which are the important parts? It all depends on the purpose of the notes.

Read students the witness report of an incident below and then select the appropriate task.

Witness report: Mrs Blueberry's garden

Mrs Blueberry, an eccentric and lovable retired teacher, was asked by the police to write a detailed witness statement about an incident she witnessed in her garden. She slightly misunderstood the task and included many details which were nothing to do with the actual incident.

'Well, I was baking a cherry pie and had just made sure I had enough custard and cream in the fridge. I am always in a good mood when I'm baking. My psychologist tells me it is good for lifting mood. So that I don't forget things I write everything down. For example, the shortcrust pastry required two and a half cups of flour, one teaspoon of salt, two tablespoons of sugar, one cup of butter and half a cup of water.

Anyway, I heard a terrible noise outside my cottage. I dashed out. Well, when I say 'dashed' I mean I went as fast as my old legs could take me. I'm 80 you know and the doctors tell me to be careful with my hip replacement. Apparently hip replacements usually need renewing after ten years and mine is well due for that, I can tell you.

I got out in the fresh air and believe it or not was out of breath. I stood panting for a few seconds and I couldn't help noticing the clouds. They were low level, about 2,000 metres I should say and as those types of clouds contain water droplets I thought we might be in for a spot of rain. Anyway, where was I? Oh yes, the noise. Well would you believe it? An army helicopter had apparently flown too low and hit a power cable and had to make an emergency landing in my garden! Well can you imagine how Hector, that's my cat, reacted? She ran like fury and hid under the shed. Cats hate noises you know, especially the noise of a Gazelle helicopter landing in your garden. Well, the soldiers, they were SAS soldiers, the elite soldiers of the British Army who go on special missions, they loved my cherry pie. I could not believe how much cream and custard they had with it. I thought it would be a good idea to make them a nice cup of tea because they'd had a rather nasty shock. They were very nice young men and one of them, with his blond hair and blue eyes, reminded me of my grandson.

Apparently, in a situation like this, the procedure is to call the police and the Military Police. Military Police only deal with matters concerning the armed forces. Now the next part of my statement is hard to believe but I swear to you that it is true. All my life I have wanted to go for a ride in a helicopter and I asked the men if that would be possible. They looked at each other, and whether it was the cherry pie or something I really don't know, but they agreed. They said they would have to check that the helicopter was in good condition and then whosh! – off we went. They asked me where I wanted to go and I said how about my sister in Brighton. Well it wasn't long before we were in my sister's garden eating her cherry pie and drinking her tea. What a day!

I've heard that the soldiers got into a tiny bit of trouble over what happened that day – but not too much. You see the SAS are very highly respected. The funny thing is that I have told my story quite a few times and nobody seems to believe me. Oh well, I know it's true and that's what matters. People say that when you're 80 you have to think back years for great memories. Well I don't. I only have to think back to a few days ago when I was flying high with the British Army. And do you know what I told my psychologist the other day? I told him that if you want to lift your mood, don't worry about baking cherry pies, just wait for an SAS helicopter to land in your garden!'

Activities

E Highlight

Ask students to read the headings in the 'Notes and summary chart' and to assign a colour to each header with a highlighter. Then ask them to reread Mrs Blueberry's incident report and highlight sections that fall under the different headings with the corresponding colour.

M Key point notes

Ask students to re-read the incident report and to write key point notes in the relevant part of the 'Notes and summary chart'. Tell them they can copy word for word from the text but if they can use their own words then that would be even better.

C Summaries

Ask students to re-read the incident report and then write a summary of the main points that the Military Police would be concerned with, in the summary box at the end of the 'Notes and summary chart'.

Notes and summary chart

Things that can improve a mood
A way to remember things
Ingredients for shortcrust pastry
Information concerning hip replacement operations
Characteristics about rain clouds
Things that cats don't like
Procedure to be followed when an army helicopter makes an emergency landing
Summary of key points prepared for the Military Police

Plenary

Using various types of notes

Using the texts from the main part of the lesson ask students to work in small groups and experiment with the various types of note taking forms listed in the table below. For your information the level of the different forms of note taking are also listed; you may want to ask certain groups of students to only focus on certain types of note taking.

Different types of note taking

Title	Level
Key notes and summary	Medium
Flow diagram: time order	Medium
Notes with drawing, symbol and only one sentence	Challenging
Triangle notes	Easy
Circle notes	Easy
From mountain to kennel	Challenging

Give students the worksheets below (also available online) and tell them that each of the types of note taking have different purposes and to make sure they read and understand these purposes before giving the note taking style a go.

Key notes and summary

Main purpose: to pick out key points and turn them into a summary.

Process: Key points are written in the left hand column in the form of words and short phrases. Then a summary of the whole text is written in the right hand box.

Key notes: (words and phrases)	Summary of whole text
• • •	

Flow diagram: time order

Main purpose: to pick out key points and present them in the same order as the original text.

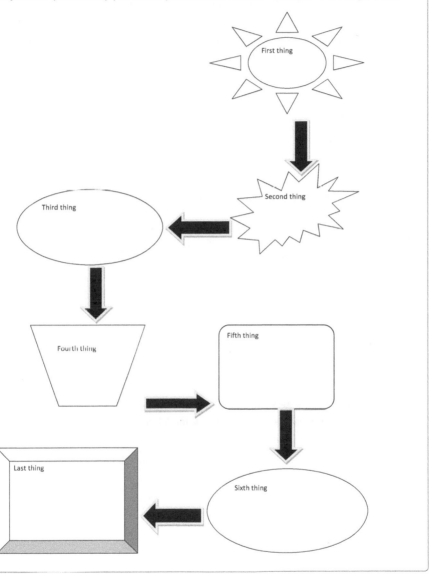

Notes with drawing, symbol and only one sentence

Main purpose: to try to express the main idea of the text as a drawing and/or a symbol and then to express the whole idea of the text as only one sentence.

Sketch a quick drawing here that to you summarises the whole text.	Draw a symbol here that to you summarises the whole text.

Write only one sentence here which summarises the whole text.

_____

_____

_____

_____

_____

Triangle notes

Main purpose: to organise information by importance by noting most important information at the top of the triangle and least important near the base.

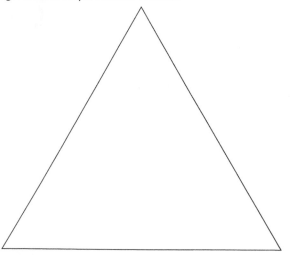

Circle notes

Main purpose: *to organise information by importance by noting important information inside or the circle and less important information outside the circle.*

From mountain to kennel

Main purpose: *to organise information by importance by noting the most important information underneath the mountain, decreasing so that the least important information sits under the kennel.*

When the class have had some time to experiment with the note taking resources draw them all together and instigate a class discussion around the following topics by displaying the following chart on the board:

What would you say are some of the difficulties we have when we write good notes?	Have you got any ideas about how we can overcome these difficulties?

Ask for contributions from the whole class and jot their comments on the chart.

Teacher's tip

A great follow up homework is for students to try to invent their own charts and methods of note taking.

Starter

Varieties of non-fiction texts

Just right for lessons when the objective is to investigate the variety of non-fiction texts.

Materials required: various colours of sticky notes.

Explain to students that there are a wide variety of non-fiction texts and this starter will explore some of them. Display the 'Varieties of non-fiction map' on the board.

Varieties of non-fiction map

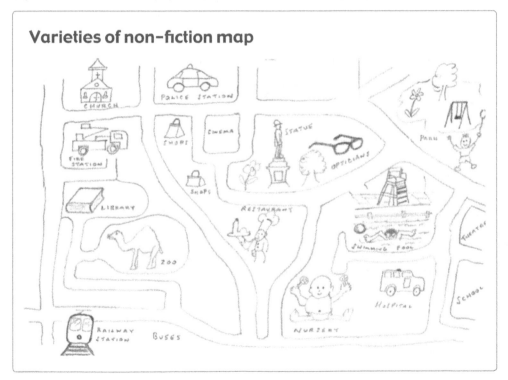

Arrange the class into groups of four and provide each group with a different coloured set of sticky notes so that it is obvious whose comments are whose.

Select the appropriate activity from the following page and ask the group to write their ideas down on their sticky notes and then to attach the notes on the suitable part of the map.

Activities

ⓔ Types of non-fiction text

Ask students to write examples of the type of text which would be typically found at the various locations on the map, then ask them to stick them on the map in the relevant places. For example, at the fire station there may be a non-fiction notice to warn people not to park in front of the fire station.

ⓜ Purposes and typical examples of content

Ask students to write down the type of text which would be usually found at the various locations and describe the purpose of the text and, if they can, add examples of the sorts of things the text would normally contain. They then place their sticky notes on the map. For example, at the zoo, near the enclosures, there may be information signs to inform visitors about the animals they are looking at; the text would normally contain things like: name of animal, photo, map, habitat details, threats.

ⓒ Styles of writing

Ask students to write down the type of text which would usually be found at the various locations on the map and briefly describe the purpose of the text and examples of the sorts of things the text would normally contain. In addition to this, ask them to have a go at writing a small example of how the text would be written. For example, at the statue there may be a brass plate describing who the statue commemorates; the text would normally contain maybe a name and who donated the statue; an example of wording might be: 'In memory of Sir William Bertie Younger born February 18th 1906 close to this spot. Donated to the city by The Federation of Master Bakers'.

Teacher's tips

- It works well if you select a group leader for each group and have a clear rule that only the leaders from each group may put the notes on the board – this eases congestion.

- You will find that it quickly engages the attention of the group if the map is displayed as the students come in and you can direct their attention to the map and start talking about non-fiction texts straight away. The colour coded sticky notes allow you to see at a glance how the various groups are progressing.

- If students require ideas and prompts, examples can be found online for all levels of activities.

Plenary

Reflecting on variety of non-fiction texts

Ask students to review the variety of non-fiction forms that they have studied in the main part of the lesson.

Provide them with the 'Variety of non-fiction chart' below, and ask them to fill it in as far as they can.

Suggestions for the different levels:

E Complete columns 1 and 2.

M Complete columns 1, 2 and 3.

C Complete columns 1, 2, 3 and 4.

Variety of non-fiction chart

1. Type of text	2. Purpose of text	3. Elements normally included	4. Examples of the style of writing

Teacher's tip

Students may wish to refer to an example of a completed chart to help guide their responses, which can be found online. A couple of examples are shown below.

1. Type	2. Purpose of text	3. Elements normally included	4. Examples of the style of writing
Notice	To give people information or to give warnings	Opening times Who to enquire to	Church notice: 'All enquiries concerning baptisms, weddings and burials to be made to the registrar (phone number provided)'
Information board (Electronic)	To show customers information which is constantly changing	Arrival and departure times	Railway Station: '17:30 Platform 12 CLACTON ON SEA Now boarding'

Starter

Features of non-fiction: auction entry forms

Suitable for when you want to prepare the students for considering the features of non-fiction texts.

Ask students to work in mixed ability groups of four, and call them group A, B, C and D. Give them a copy of ' The account of Geoff's accident' and the 'Non-fiction auction entry form'.

Note: The actual auction will be held at the end as a plenary but the starter will be used to complete the form.

Read the class 'The account of Geoff's accident'. In their groups, ask them to discuss the different types of non-fiction texts listed on the auction form and the features they might contain, and then to tick the relevant boxes.

The account of Geoff's accident

A situation like this can involve a variety of non-fiction texts.

On Thursday 12 January 2012, Geoff Monk was excited to purchase his dream car, a 1959 Peugeot model 403. The sun was shining and he felt on top of the world as he indicated to turn left into the High Street. Then something terrible happened. The car, his pride and joy which he had paid £8,000 for and had owned for barely an hour, suffered a broken steering rod and Geoff, though he frantically struggled, completely lost control of the car and found himself smashed against the corner window of a large department store. Luckily, nobody was injured but you can imagine how the frightened pedestrians leaped out of the way.

Below is an example of part of the auction form (the full form is online).

Type of non-fiction text	Reason for using it	Non-fiction features you would normally expect to see. Tick the relevant ones.				
1. Advert for the car in the local paper	The police wanted to see if the advert referred to an MOT test certificate.	Heading	Table of contents	Index	Bold print	Information box
		Photo	Diagram	Chart	Date	Signature
		Caption	Table	Map	Quotation	Persuasive language
		A column of figures	Official headed paper	A letter form	Statistical information	Technical words
		Phone number	Address	A warning clause	Label	Subheading
		Facts	Italics	Coloured font	A key	Contents page
2. Receipt for the car	The police wanted to ensure that Geoff was the legal owner.	Heading	Table of contents	Index	Bold print	Information box
		Photo	Diagram	Chart	Date	Signature
		Caption	Table	Map	Quotation	Persuasive language
		A column of figures	Official headed paper	A letter form	Statistical information	Technical words
		Phone number	Address	A warning clause	Label	Subheading
		Facts	Italics	Coloured font	A key	Contents page
3. MOT Certificate for the car	The police wanted to see if the steering was checked.	Heading	Table of contents	Index	Bold print	Information box
		Photo	Diagram	Chart	Date	Signature
		Caption	Table	Map	Quotation	Persuasive language
		A column of figures	Official headed paper	A letter form	Statistical information	Technical words
		Phone number	Address	A warning clause	Label	Subheading
		Facts	Italics	Coloured font	A key	Contents page
4. Police Forensic Report on the car	The police wanted to find out exactly what had gone wrong and why.	Heading	Table of contents	Index	Bold print	Information box
		Photo	Diagram	Chart	Date	Signature
		Caption	Table	Map	Quotation	Persuasive language
		A column of figures	Official headed paper	A letter form	Statistical information	Technical words
		Phone number	Address	A warning clause	Label	Subheading
		Facts	Italics	Coloured font	A key	Contents page

Remind students that they must be careful to justify their choices because in the auction, which will take place at the end of the lesson, you may do a spot check to see if their responses are reasonable and they will be asked to say why they made their choices. Warn students that they risk being disqualified from the auction if they've inflated the number of ticks.

Teacher's tips

At first the students might find it hard to imagine the various non-fiction texts and what their features might be. Two useful tips are:

- Get them started by prompting them with a few examples. The more they start engaging with the activity, the more ideas will come to them.

- Make them feel comfortable about experimenting and making reasonable guesses. An important point at this stage is to encourage students to freely contribute. Walk round the room and listen to the discussions going on in the groups. If they call out things which are wrong, be particularly careful with the language you use which must be designed to encourage, teach and guide. For example: 'No, Charlie that might not be right but you'll soon get the flow of it as we go along. Keep your contributions going...'

Plenary

Reflecting on the features of non-fiction: the auction

Prepare for the auction:

1. Arrange the room like an auction room.

2. Display a score board.

3. Bring in an auctioneer's hammer.

4. Ask a student to be your assistant to act as scorer.

Tell students to sit in their groups (A,B,C and D allocated in the starter) ready for the auction. They will need their completed 'Non-fiction auction entry forms.' Explain to the students that you will act as the auctioneer and you will work your way down the list, auctioning off the different types of non-fiction text. Your students will use their ticks to 'buy' the items, so the group with the most correct ticks will end up winning the item. Use the first item as a test run to ensure everyone understands the process. Below are some examples:

Auction examples

The auctioneer starts with the first non-fiction item on the sheet, calling out: 'I start the bidding for the item listed as number one, the advert for the car in the local paper, starting the bidding at two features. Any advance on two features? (Students shout out advances.) Three, four, five do I hear six? Six features anybody? And seven to the gentleman in the corner. Eight anybody, eight … I see nine goes to the girl here at the front. Nine features ticked for the advert for the car, going, going … gone. (Hammer comes down dramatically.) Sold! To the girl at the front. Scorer please enter nine points for group A please. Now, we are ready to start the bidding for item listed as number 2 in your brochure…'

Every now and then, do a quality control in a lively upbeat way. This is a great way to learn. Here is a small example:

'Now, just a moment, I want to do a spot check quality control on your entry form please sir. Now then, let's see. You've got five boxes ticked for the blood test report. Oh, well I think they're OK except perhaps for this one. I don't think you should have ticked the 'quotation box' for a blood test report on driver. That would be more for a newspaper for example. But the others seem fine. Well done.'

Teacher's tips

- Before starting the auction, to help it run smoothly and to give it a professional feel, ask students to add up their ticks and write their totals in the margin. It is important that you give them enough time to carefully check their totals to avoid arguments and confusion in the heat of the auction room.

- One of the common things that can go wrong with this is for the students to bid too high too quickly and that messes up the flow and build up of tension. Before the auction starts it is worth explaining this to the students and asking them to only put their hand up when the bidding reaches their level, and not before.

- It is a good idea to keep the same groups as you had in the starter and give each one a paddle with their group letter on it so that the bidder can hold up their number when the hammer comes down, just like in a real auction.

- The idea can of course be adapted for other texts you may be studying and other features you need to identify and discuss.

Starter

Fact or opinion

Ideal for lessons that investigate the difference between fact and opinion.

Materials required: blood-stained carpet (red ink on a small piece of carpet); scattered books; piece of sock; damaged shoe; broken clock; battery from broken clock; screwed up note. Alternatively, adapt the text below and use other objects of your own choice.

Before the students arrive for the lesson, lay the items around the room as described in the text 'Mr Higgin's break in', with chairs set out surrounding the scene. As the students walk in and sit down direct their attention to the props on the floor with intriguing phrases such as 'Don't touch those! The full forensic team will be along soon to examine them. We've got to try to work out what happened here last night. Sit down please.'

When all the class are seated read them the following text:

Mr Higgins' break in

Mr Higgins' break in, 1 August 2011 (substitute for today's date) 14 Gobbold Road, Cranleigh, Surrey.

Good morning everybody. I'm Inspector *(your surname)* and I'm going to explain to you what we know so far. You see that piece of cloth lying near that sideboard, well, we think that is what the burglar used to put on Mr Higgins' mouth to render him unconscious. Don't worry, Mr Higgins is being cared for by a neighbour right now. He is a little shocked but otherwise he's fine! Nothing can be moved, even a tiny bit, until the full forensic team have done their work. The 'interim tests' have been done on some items already to give us a bit of a head start. I've sniffed that cloth and I think it's got chloroform on it, although I can't be sure at this stage.

You see that clock, on its side over there. Well that is a vital clue. It fell off the sideboard, probably in the scuffle, and when it hit the floor the battery came out, as you can see. The time shown on it is 2.15 a.m. so that is how we know when all this took place.

We've got a hunch that the thief had broken in, shall we say at about 2 a.m., and was rummaging around when Mr Higgins' dog woke up and started barking. Mr Higgins came downstairs and confronted the burglar and that is when the burglar forced the cloth on

---

to Mr Higgins' mouth to make him unconscious. The dog probably turned on the thief at that point and the thief clouted the dog round the head with that statuette over there. But that didn't stop the dog from biting his shoe off, together with a chunk of his sock. It seems as if the burglar then made a sharp exit out of the window there! The dog's OK but the poor old thing has got a bit of a bump on its head.

Now, you'll also notice that scattered in that area over there are quite a few books. We think the burglar was searching for something, probably cash, which he guessed might be stashed somewhere.

Now here's an interesting thing. You see that dark brown stain on the carpet over by the window? Well, we've already had an interim report on that and it is definitely human blood. It is not Mr Higgins' blood, we know that, so we assume it is from the burglar. There are no traces on the broken window, as you'd expect, so we're not sure exactly how he came to cut himself. If you're thinking that the dog did it I'm afraid you're on the wrong track there. The dog's mouth has been tested and there appears to be no trace.

Here's another interesting thing. We found this screwed up note which must have fallen from the burglar's pocket in the scuffle. If you look up at the screen you'll see that it's a kind of plan of the neighbourhood and you can clearly see that he has put a red cross at this property. This is a vital clue as it shows his hand writing. Unfortunately though, there are no fingerprints. He must have worn gloves.

Now we come to the puzzling part of the thing that has us all baffled! The contents have all been checked with Mr Higgins and he can confirm that nothing whatsoever has been stolen except this. If you look at the screen you will see it is an old postcard. The reason he can be so sure is that he has just had everything listed for insurance purposes and everything in the house has been photographed and valued. This particular postcard has been insured for £10,000 and we have absolutely no idea how the burglar would have known that. Most of Mr Higgins' postcards (and he has a vast collection) are valued at about a pound or so.

I wonder if you could help us. In order to start to sort things out we need to know what is fact and what is opinion, to stop us getting confused and to help us write out our reports for when it eventually goes to court, that is, if we can catch him. Could you fill out the chart?

Ask the students to fill in the 'Fact and opinion chart' with ticks and comments. This works well across the ability range. The students can work on the chart individually or in small groups.

Teacher's tip

The whole idea is to stimulate discussion about the difference between facts and opinions and identify grey areas that sit between the two. You will find that the scattering of props on the floor is an unusual and intriguing sight for the students as they enter the room and will help greatly to immediately spark their interest and draw in their attention. The mystery element will stimulate their creative imaginations. It may be useful to have a copy of the text you have read out for students to refer to as they fill in the chart.

Fact and opinion chart

Information	A definite fact	Need more information to establish as a definite fact	A definite opinion	Not sure
1. The cloth had chloroform on it.				
2. Mr Higgins is shocked by the incident.				
3. The full forensic team are on their way.				
4. The forensic team are the best in the world.				
5. The clock stopped working in the scuffle.				
6. The dog bit the burglar's shoe off.				
7. Mr Higgins acted in the right way.				
8. The books were scattered on the floor.				
9. The reason that the books were scattered is because the burglar was searching for something.				

Information	A definite fact	Need more information to establish as a definite fact	A definite opinion	Not sure
10. The blood stain is human blood.				
11. The blood stain is from the burglar.				
12. The rough street plan contains some wonderful handwriting.				
13. The rough street plan has no fingerprints on it.				
14. The postcard was worth £10,000.				
15. The reason the burglar didn't take anything else is because he was disturbed by the dog.				

Plenary

Reviewing fact or opinion

Materials required: 12 x 4 pieces of A4 card each in 4 different colours: red, blue, orange and green. The colours represent the following:

Red: fact

Blue: opinion

Orange: could be a fact but need more information

Green: not sure if it is a fact or an opinion

Ask 12 students to stand at the front of the class. Give each of them a pack of the 4 different coloured cards. To each of the 12 students also distribute cards with short extracts on them taken from the text studied in the main part of the lesson. Ask the first student to read out their card. The rest of the class then have to vote whether the extract is red, blue, orange or green and the 12 students at the front all display the coloured card that the majority have voted for.

So for example, one of the 12 students reads out:

'She was the most beautiful woman alive!'

The teacher then calls out each option and the class (not the including the 12 at the front) votes by a show of hands. If 'opinion' wins the vote then all the 12 students at the front will hold up the blue A4 cards to denote 'opinion'. When all 12 students are holding up their cards, the physical sight of the students standing at the front with coloured cards makes the exercise visually powerful. The student then re-reads the extract to confirm and reinforce what it is. As the class hear the extract a second time they are looking at the powerful display of students holding the blue opinion cards. This will drive home the points being made and provoke a discussion if the wrong colour has been voted for previously.

Teacher's tips

- It is a good idea, during this process, to have the key to the colours displayed on the board as a reminder.

- It works well if you prepare a supply of extracts of various kinds, taken from the materials studied in the main body of the lesson, to match all four categories and have them printed out on small cards. If you ask the students to select examples themselves you will find that you quickly run out of time and the key to a good plenary is to keep it brisk and dynamic.

Section 5
Speaking and listening

Starter

Top tips for presentation

Good for preparing students to give a spoken presentation to the class.

Arrange the class so that there is plenty of room at the front for the speaker to move about and organise their exhibits and visuals. Prepare the help cards below.

Explain to students that the ability to give a good spoken presentation is something that can be learnt and improved with practice. Presenting well is a vital skill to learn and is especially valuable in the workplace because if you are good at presenting you will be more effective at clearly expressing your ideas and therefore you will allow people to understand more powerfully and clearly what you are saying. Remind students that the important thing is not just what is actually said but also the way the information is presented.

The starter exercise is a fun experiment. The idea is to start off with a rather plain and uninspiring presentation which then has improvements made layer by layer, using students from the audience who can see the techniques improving before their eyes. Start off by asking three students to volunteer to stand up in front of the class and read a short presentation.

Ask volunteer 1 to read 'Help card 1'.

Help card 1

Instructions to reader: Put your head down and speak in a low, barely audible monotone voice, with no pauses. Clench your fists and act as though you are feeling tense as you speak.

There are many kinds of fishing. There is freshwater and sea. I do sea. I have rods and reels and nets and bait. I go with my dad and we take sandwiches and a flask. We are part of a club and we like fishing. We have caught lots of different kinds of fish. I have been fishing for a long time and my dad has been fishing even longer. When you catch the fish you have to gut it and I know how to do that. Once I cut my finger. I bought my equipment from the fishing tackle shop and it is quite new. I want to buy a new rod. I have got two more rods at home. The line is 54 lb which is quite strong. We go at night and in the rain but I like it best in the summer because it is warm. I want to do a lot more fishing with my dad.

When the volunteer has finished reading the card, ask the audience what they thought of the presentation. Why was the presentation uninspiring?

Give volunteer 2 'Help card 2' and ask them to present it as directed by the instructions on the card. The focus here is how the presentation is engaging at the opening due to the use of quotes.

Help card 2

(Look at the audience, open you arms in an engaging way and smile.) 'Have you ever wondered why fishing is one of the most popular pastimes in the world?' *(Pause and look at the audience in anticipation.)* 'Well, I'd like to read you a couple of quotes from people who loved fishing. A man called Washington Irving, who died over 150 years ago, said 'There is certainly something in fishing that tends to produce a gentleness of spirit and a pure serenity of the mind.' *(Look at the audience, pause for a second and then say)* 'what a lovely way to say 'relaxing'...a pure serenity of mind.' *(Now stand up straight and breath in dramatically and say)* 'but fishing can also be incredibly exciting. Listen to what a Hollywood stunt man said about catching a shark off California 'For over an hour we battled! The shark pulled my boat along and every time I tried to reel it in I thought my rod would snap! In the end I did land it in the boat and we struggled together in pure exhaustion. After a quick photograph I chucked it back, unharmed. It was quite simply, the most exciting buzz I've ever had...and I earn a living as a stunt man!'

Ask the class if they thought this presentation was more engaging. If so, why?

Ask volunteer 3 to present 'Help card 3'. The focus here is the middle part of the presentation which uses visualisation.

Help card 3

(Stand nice and confidently and calmly and smile at your audience. Take your time. Maintain positive eye contact.) 'Now, why do I love fishing so much? In order to answer that I would like you all to do something for me which will only take a few moments but hopefully will be quite enjoyable.' *(Pause, and look confidently at your audience.)* 'Close your eyes, gently. I want you to imagine something. You are camping on a warm summer's evening and sitting with your best friend by the side of a calm, beautiful river which reflects the orange and pink light of the sky. The air is fresh and clean and sweet. In the distance are graceful mountains with forests snuggled in the valleys. Beside you is a camp fire and sizzling in a frying pan is a trout which you have just caught and prepared. Very soon it will be ready for you to bite into the succulent tender fish and taste the flavour enhanced by the herbs which you found earlier that day. The end of your rod rings a small bell and you prepare to reel in the next trout.' *(Now pause and allow people to open their eyes. Hold the pause.)* 'That's why I love fishing. I know that is a dream situation but as the great poet Browning said 'your dream must always be beyond your reach – or what's a heaven for?'

Ask the students if they thought this presentation was more engaging. If so, why did they think that?

Teacher's tips

- Remember to guide the class carefully through the steps so that they can see the gradual improvements taking place. Thank the students, particularly the student who started by reading card I for doing a good job in presenting a deliberately uninspiring presentation which is vital so that the improvements can be measured against it. To keep the pace of this dynamic starter going it is important to quickly brief the volunteers, one at a time and run through the highlights of their help card, before they give the presentation.

- Creating an atmosphere of fun, work in progress and experimentation is the key atmosphere to aim for. The volunteers who come up and present will not give whole presentations but merely small samples to illustrate various points and techniques. Explain to the class that 'fishing' as the content of the presentations is just an example and that the main point of the lesson is that the presentation techniques they are learning can be applied to any subject. Good presentation skills can make any subject interesting for the audience!

- Online and in the following plenary, is a worksheet called 'Presentation tips' offering extensive advice on how to give a good presentation.

Plenary

Using the best tips

Once the students have worked out roughly what their individual presentations will be about in the main part of the lesson, arrange for a few volunteers to present their work in progress to the class. The rest of the class will use their 'Presentation tips' sheet (see below) to comment on areas they thought were good and areas that could possibly be enhanced a little.

Presentation tips

Tip	Tick	Comment
1. Make sure that the steps of your presentation are clear for the audience to follow.		
2. Maintain eye contact with your audience to engage them. Do not stare at people but look at someone and then shift your gaze to another part of the audience. Do not stare at the wall above the heads of the audience as this makes you look like a robot!		
3. If you have a visual display, like a picture on a PowerPoint, look at it briefly but then look back at the audience. If you look at the visual for too long you will lose some of the interest of the audience.		
4. Rehearse, rehearse, rehearse! The more you prepare and rehearse the better the presentation will be.		
5. Don't keep talking without a pause. Get into the habit of pausing after you have given some information, to let it sink in. Your audience will really appreciate that. In most presentations the speakers speak too fast and do not pause. It makes the audience tense. You want to arouse the interest of the audience and engage them but you do not want to make them tense.		
5. Practice even breathing before you start to make yourself calmer. If you can, try humming a little as this vibrates the vocal cords and lowers the pitch of your voice and therefore makes it more pleasant to listen to. Do what actors do and clench your fists and count to three then release them to relax the body.		

Tip	Tick	Comment
6. Try to make your voice loud and powerful without shouting. One of the biggest problems with public speaking is that the audience can not hear.		
7. Try to sound interested and enthusiastic about the subject. If you do this you will automatically engage your audience more effectively. (But don't over-do it!)		
8. Hold small cards in your hand with one word or short phrases for key point reminders. You can then casually glance down to the top of the pack to remind yourself of the next point and put that card to the back of the pack. It is vital that you rehearse the use of these prompt cards to give your presentation a polished and smooth feel to it. The key word on the card must 'trigger' something which you know really well.		
9. Don't give too much detailed information as this will bore your audience. Simplify things and present them in an upbeat way. Think of the style of adverts rather than documentaries. Use interesting relevant quotes. Read them but keep them short. If you can remember them that would be great.		
10. If you use a PowerPoint be certain that you have run through the presentation all the way from switching it on to making sure it all works correctly and smoothly. Have a plan B if the PowerPoint stops working. Untold thousands of presentations have been ruined by people fumbling helplessly with laptops and PowerPoints. There is no quicker way to aggravate and alienate an audience. Also make sure that you use pictures and large keywords. Never use small font and never just read it!		
11. Use a flip chart with dark coloured pens because you can talk about things as you briefly write them up and this locks in interest.		
12. If you use a prop or an object don't just show them, build anticipation and then show them. Don't pass the prop around until the end of the presentation. If you have handouts, never give them out during the presentation as the audience will shift their attention from you to the handout. However, if you can find short and lively fun ways to involve the audience that can work brilliantly.		

Tip	Tick	Comment
13. Enrich your language and bring it alive by telling short punchy stories; use similes and metaphors; find out about rhetorical devices like the rule of three and repetition; 'paint visual pictures' with words and consider enriching the experience by playing short extracts of music to allow the audience to visualise a scene as you softly speak over the background music.		
14. At the end sincerely thank your audience for listening and invite questions.		

Teacher's tip

Point out that these are 'interim' presentations and the 'Presentation tips' sheet will give the students some specific advice to take home and work on as they practice and improve their presentations. Create an atmosphere which allows all the students to help each other improve.

Starter

Body language games

A great starter for lessons where the focus is on body language during presentations.

Explain to the class that when we give a talk it isn't just the words we use which gets the message across. 70% of our message and meaning is communicated through body language. Body language includes things like the expression on our face, the way we stand, hand gestures, movements and many other things. Tell the class that you are going to have a little game to get them thinking about body language. The game will be in two parts.

Part 1: Scenarios without words

Read the scenarios below to the whole class and also project the words onto a screen. Then ask for volunteers to come to the front and to act out the scenarios using the body language that would be employed in the different situations.

Body language scenarios

Note: The number in brackets at the end of each scenario indicates the number of volunteers required.

1. Someone has come home after a hard day at school. They are in a bad mood. They slump down onto a chair and then hold the pose of tiredness and exhaustion. (1)

2. A person is sitting at a restaurant table absolutely famished. She is expecting a hearty meal and can't wait. The waiter brings her a plate with a few pieces of lettuce and a hard-boiled egg. She looks at the plate and then holds the pose of shocked disgust. (2)

3. A person knocks on a door and the person who opens it is expecting to greet a special visitor and is very disappointed to see somebody else there. Hold the pose of a look of great disappointment. (2)

4. It is the end of a very difficult interview and the manager stands by the door (with authority) and the employee stands up and shuffles out with head down. He has been fired! Hold the pose as he reaches the door. (2)

5. Someone has been waiting to meet a famous person (perhaps they are pacing up and down). At last, the famous person enters the room. They move towards each other to shake hands. Hold the pose at the point just before they meet. (2)

6. A zookeeper opens the gate in a routine way to the elephant enclosure. She then stops and stares. Hold the pose as she realizes, incredibly, that the elephant has gone! (1)

7. A person is just about to pick up their best dress/suit and sees that the cat has been sick all over it. Hold the pose as you pick the clothes up. (1)

8. Someone hears a strange noise in the middle of the night and gets out of bed. He goes to the top of the stairs and holds the pose as he intently listens. (1)

9. Someone has been on a train for two hours and is getting drowsy. She tries to sleep but the person next to her is speaking loudly on a mobile phone. She looks across and holds the pose of utter annoyance. (2)

10. A person has saved someone's life. The rescuer is about to meet the person he rescued. The rescued person looks up. Hold the pose as their eyes meet. (2)

Teacher's tip

Make sure that there is enough space for a 'performance area' at the front of the class. It works best if the students mime the situation, to get the 'feel' of it and then run it through again and hold a pose at the end, for a few seconds, to illustrate the body language. The teacher's presence is vital here, to prompt the volunteers to hold the pose, and to remind the class what the scenario is. It works well, if after one student has performed they briskly return to their seat and another student quickly gets up to perform the next scenario. This is important for flow and rhythm which keeps interest levels up. If there is time, get the students to work out their own scenarios and body language poses for the class to guess what is happening.

Part 2: Scenarios combining words and body language

Students are to come to the front of the class and read out one of the extracts opposite to get the feel of it and then read it a second time, with appropriate body language to amplify the meaning and make it clearer.

Words and body language scenarios

1. A headteacher addresses an assembly 'I will not have bullying in my school!'

2. A person in an art gallery looks up at a painting 'Now that is a beautiful painting.'

3. A presenter introduces a champion wrestler 'Ladies and gentlemen, let's hear it for … Billy Hulkman Warrior!'

4. Someone speaks to their friend 'After all these years and all that we've been through, I never thought you would have done what you did …'

5. A clown visits a patient in a hospital to try to cheer him up 'You'll be out of this place before you know it! You'll be back to playing football before you can say one two three! Just picture walking on the beach in the sunshine, or running in the soft, sweet, fragrant rain in a forest! Come on. The doctor told me you're doing fine. You're doing fine!'

Teacher's tip

It is a good idea to demonstrate a few gestures before starting. The activity works well, if the first time the words are said they are delivered as neutrally as possible without body language; the power of body language is then exemplified by comparison when the student repeats the phrase using body language.

Plenary

Reviewing body language

After the students have delivered their presentations in the main part of the lesson, the other students are to assess the use of body language.

Activities

ⒺIdentify use of body language

Students are to make a note of a couple of examples of body language used.

ⓂHow did it help?

Students are to identify three examples of body language and to comment on why they were effective. What did the body language add to the meaning?

ⒼHow could it improve?

Students are to identify a few examples of body language used and suggest why it worked well and then offer suggestions for how it could work even better.

Teacher's tip

Ask the students to look out for and focus on the effective use of body language at the beginning of the lesson before students start to give their presentations, in preparation for this plenary activity. To focus the students' attention, it is a good idea to give them a 'Body language assessment sheet' (on the next page) for them to tick and jot down notes on as they watch the presentations. These sheets are then useful feedback tools for the presenters to consider. An example of a completed sheet can be found on online.

Body language assessment sheet

Type of body language to look out for	Comments
1. Facial expression. Does it match the meaning? Are there smiles and engaging friendly expressions?	
2. Arms and gestures. Are they used to help make the meaning clear or do they distract?	
3. Pose. Relaxed and confident or tense and uptight?	
4. Movement. Controlled and necessary or nervous and unnecessary? Does the presenter walk around too much or move in such a way to amplify meaning?	
5. Mood and attitude. Appropriate?	
6. Fidgety movements like scratching nose or keep touching watch. Can these be reduced or removed?	
7. Eyes. Engaging and looking at people for the right amount of time and then scanning the group? Does the person look nowhere in particular?	
8. Use of body language when drawing attention to props or pictures. Are the movements clear and helpful or distracting? Could this be improved?	
9. Are there barriers to communication like the presenter hiding behind a table? Should they come out to the front and use the space to help engage the audience?	

Starter

Preparation for the debate

This starter is useful for limbering up the students' debating skills.

Display statements on the board that provoke a 'for' and 'against' debate. There are 25 statements provided in a PowerPoint online, including:

Statements to debate

For just one day a year, by law, everybody should go without food so that they can understand the plight of the poor better.

It would be a good thing if there was a special pair of glasses available which, if you wore them, would allow you to read someone's thoughts.

There should be an invention so that at the age of ten you could put your head into a special scanning machine and all the world's knowledge could be transferred into your brain.

The law should allow a maximum of 6 hours sleep per person per night so that people can work more hours and make the country more productive.

If your progress at school is good the reward should be for you to be able to wear any clothes you like.

Divide the class into two teams and call them 'for' and 'against' teams. (You can alternate which team is 'for' and which is 'against' throughout the activity if you prefer.) The teacher awards points on the score board for valid points that are well presented, at their discretion.

Rules of debate:

1. Each speaker is allowed a set amount of time (30 seconds is recommended to keep the pace brisk), to speak and give their point of view without being interrupted from the other team. It is then the turn of the other side to put across their opposing view.

2. Anyone in the team can volunteer to speak but only one speaker from each team will debate each slide.

3. The teacher acts as judge and scorer and chooses who may speak next.

4. Politeness must be shown at all times.

Teacher's tips

- It is important that the teacher comments about why they are awarding points for certain comments to continually direct the thoughts of the students towards what good debating skills are and to reinforce the learning throughout the starter. It is also important to keep the pace brisk and allow one speaker for each slide and then move onto the next slide where different speakers can be chosen. If there is little response to a particular slide, it works well if the teacher suggests a couple of points to get the debate going and if there is still not much response move on to the next slide. The slides cover a wide range of debating issues.

- If a slide is evoking a particularly good debate then let it roll on a bit perhaps including other speakers from the teams.

Plenary

How could we do better?

Don't wait until the end of the lesson to do this plenary. Stop the debates going on in the main part of the lesson at key points and ask the class to fill out the 'Debate response form' (below). Ask them to share some of their findings with the class to help self-regulate and improve the quality of the debate as it progresses. They act as reminders to keep things on track and allow the management of the quality of the debate to be with the students themselves. Your role is to oversee the smooth running of the process.

Debate response form

Aspect of the debate	How could we do better? Write notes and comments here.
Voice. Is the voice calm and considered? Is it loud and clear?	
Timing. Are we spending the right time on each debating topic? Are we saying too much? Should we develop more?	
Keeping to the point. Are we keeping to the point or straying off?	
Are we using examples to support what we are saying?	
Are we being polite and respectful to opposing views?	
Are we remembering you can look at things from more than one angle?	
Are we listening well and not interrupting?	
When we speak are we using techniques to make what we say interesting to engage our audience?	
Are we learning from each other?	
Other observations.	

Teacher's tip

It is a great idea to have a blank form (available online) displayed on the board so that the teacher can quickly flag some of the key points up as the lesson progresses and as the students feedback some of their own observations.

Other titles available in the Starters and Plenaries series:

Secondary Starters and Plenaries by Kate Brown
More Secondary Starters and Plenaries by Mike Gershon
Secondary Starters and Plenaries: History by Mike Gershon

Other titles available from Bloomsbury Education:

How To Survive Your First Year in Teaching by Sue Cowley
Pimp Your Lesson! by Isabella Wallace and Leah Kirkham
Why Are You Shouting At Us? The dos and don'ts of behaviour management by Phil Beadle and John Murphy